EASY ORIGAMI

With over 60 pull-out sheets to fold

Illustrated by Teresa Bellon and Lo Cole

Written by Abigail Wheatley

Designed by Tom Ashton-Booth
and Melissa Gandhi

How to use this book

This book contains 61 tear-out sheets you can fold to make 11 different origami animals. At the back of the book you'll also find simple, step-by-step folding instructions for you to follow.

Before you fold an animal

Each sheet has folding lines printed on both sides of the paper, and bright dots to help you position the paper. Look for the animal symbol at the edge of each sheet – this tells you which folding instructions to use.

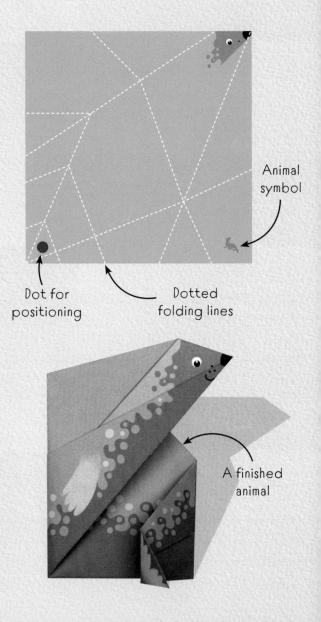

Butterfly   Bird   Fish   Dinosaur   Seal   Crocodile

Penguin   Whale   Crab   Bug   Frog

Animal symbol

Dot for positioning

Dotted folding lines

Folding

Find the folding instructions for the animal you've chosen at the back of this book. Follow each step in order. If you need more tips, you can scan a QR code to watch video clips of all the folds being made.

Helpful hints

Put the sheet flat on a table in front of you. Don't move the paper unless the instructions tell you to. Rub over each fold with the side of your thumb nail to make a sharp crease.

A finished animal

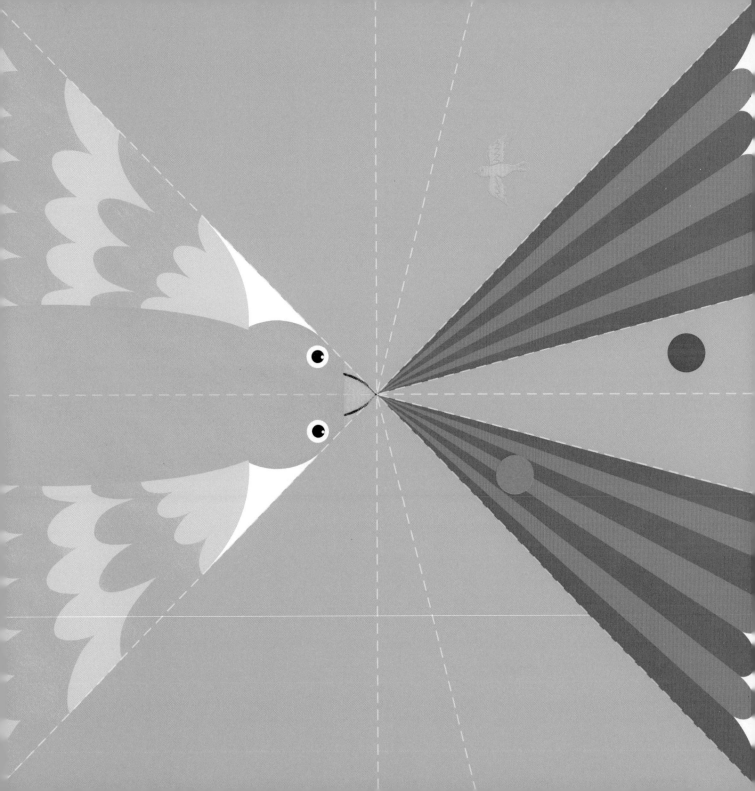

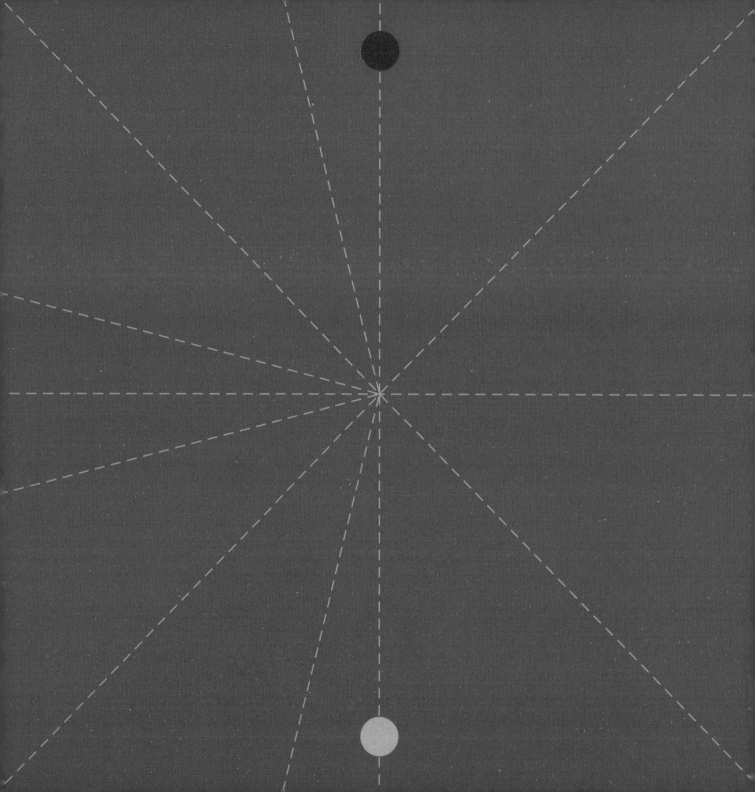

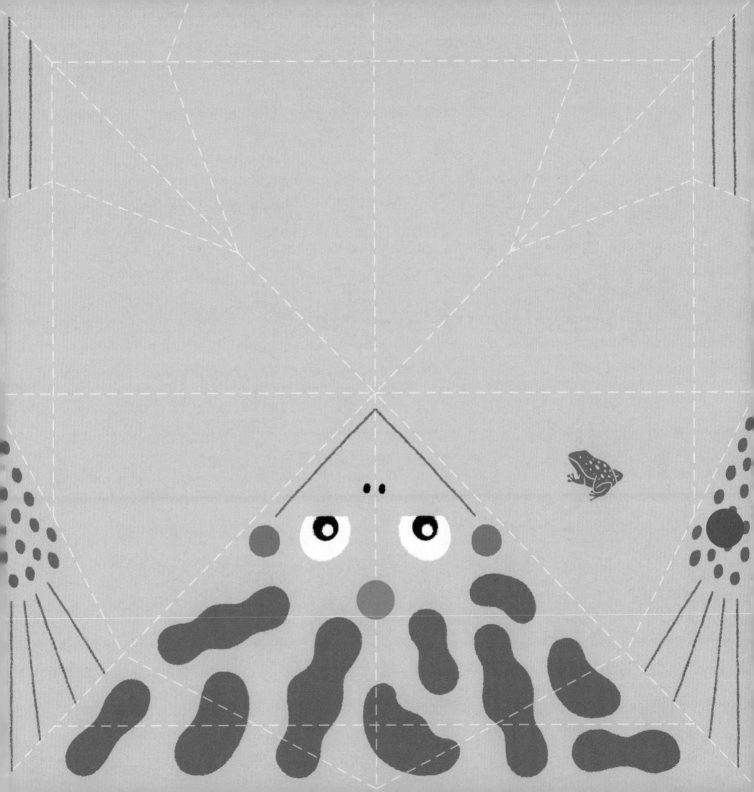

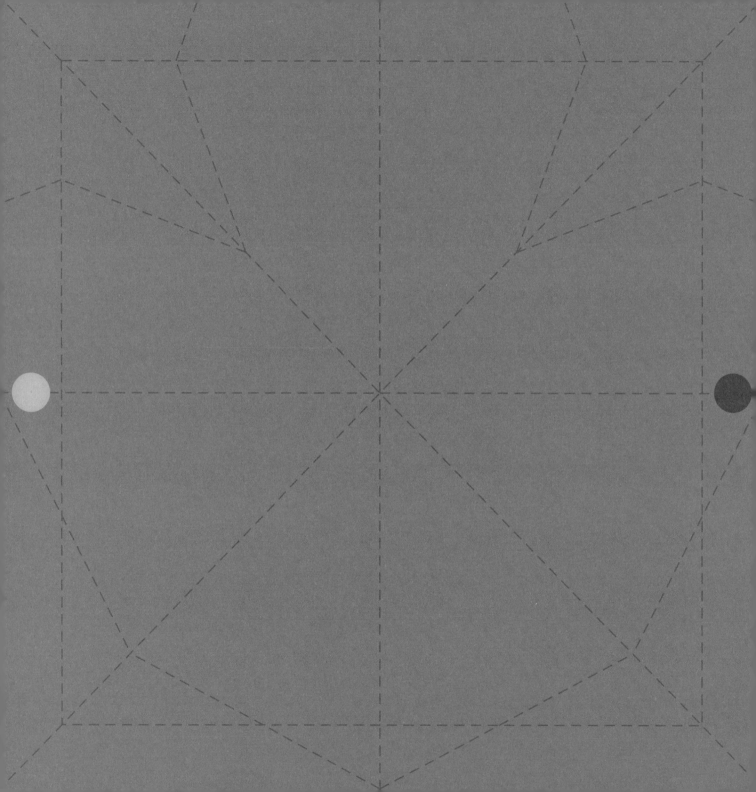

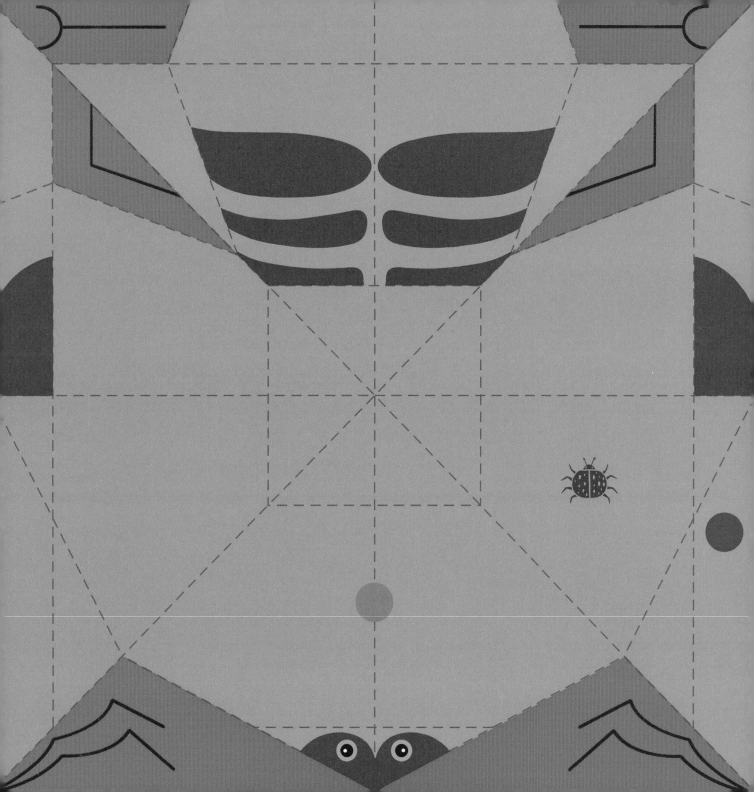

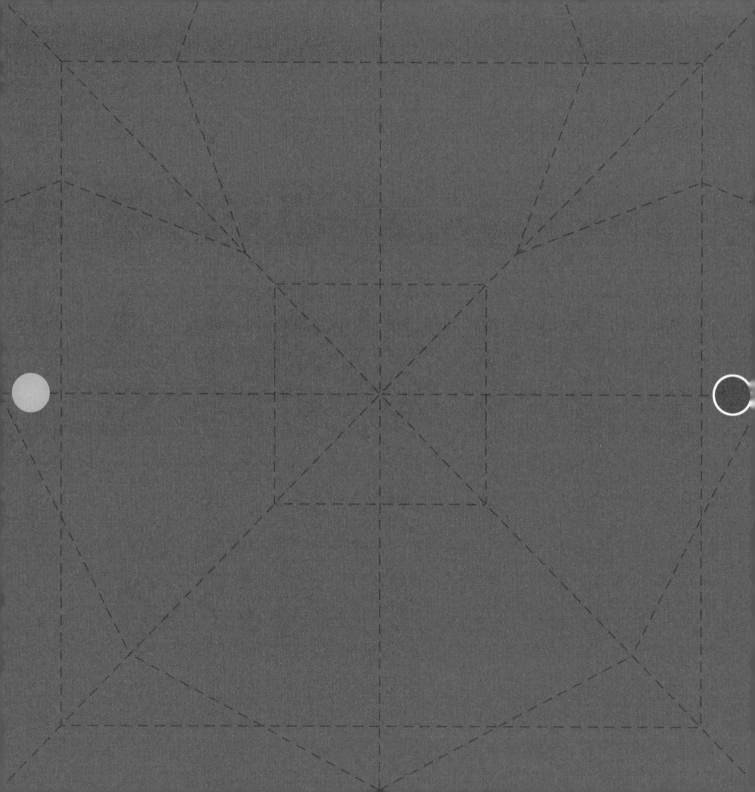

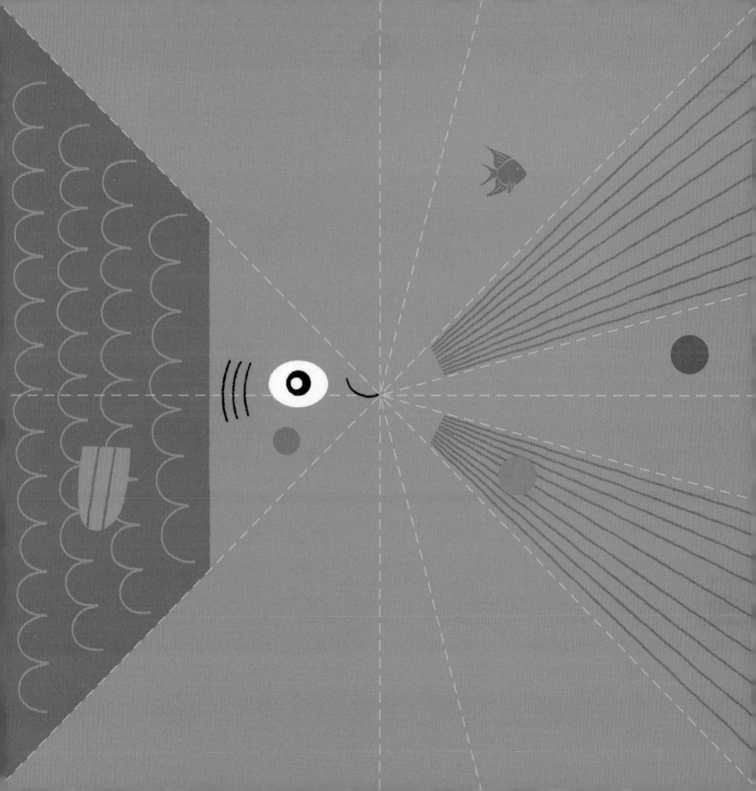

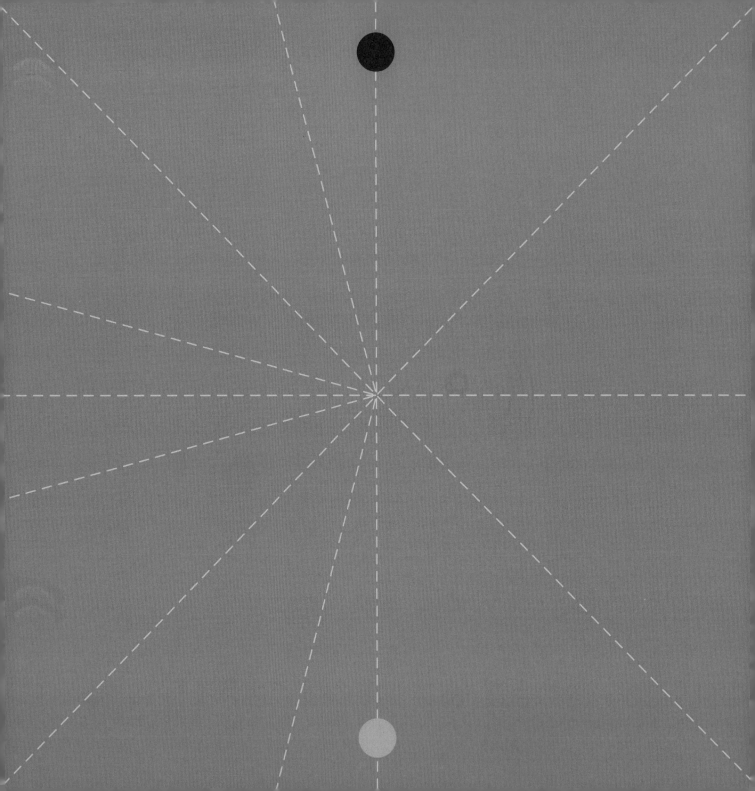

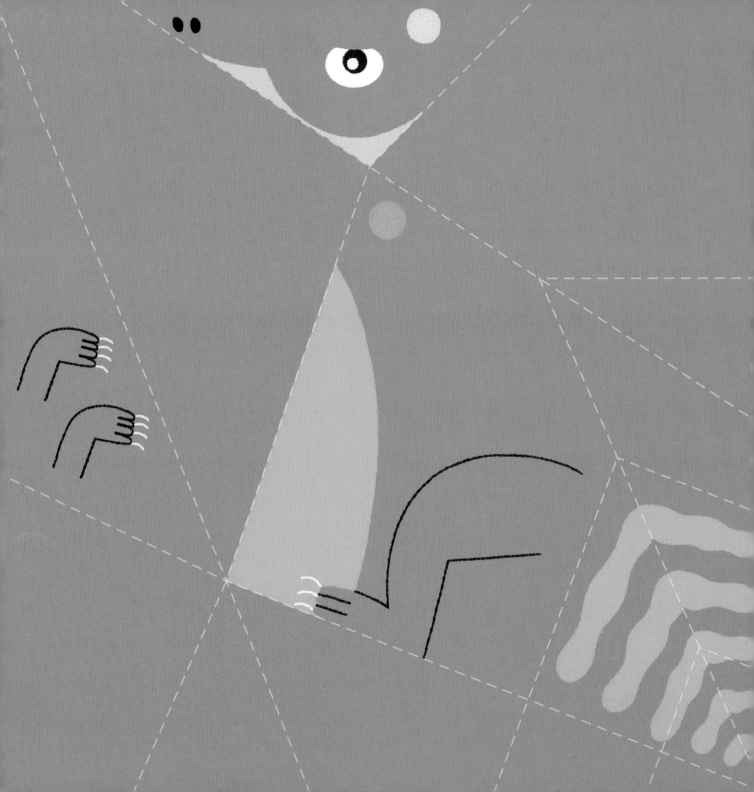

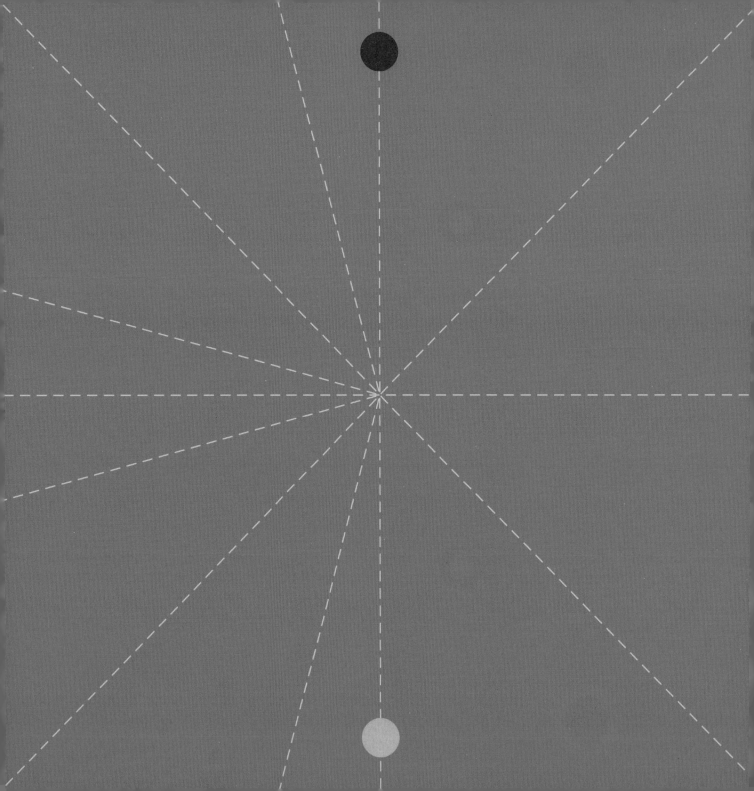

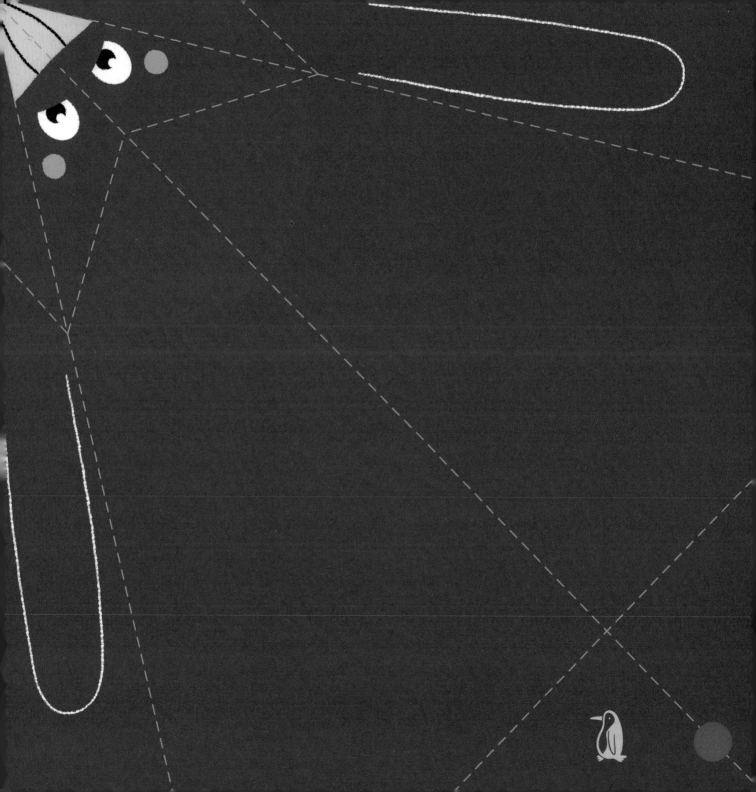

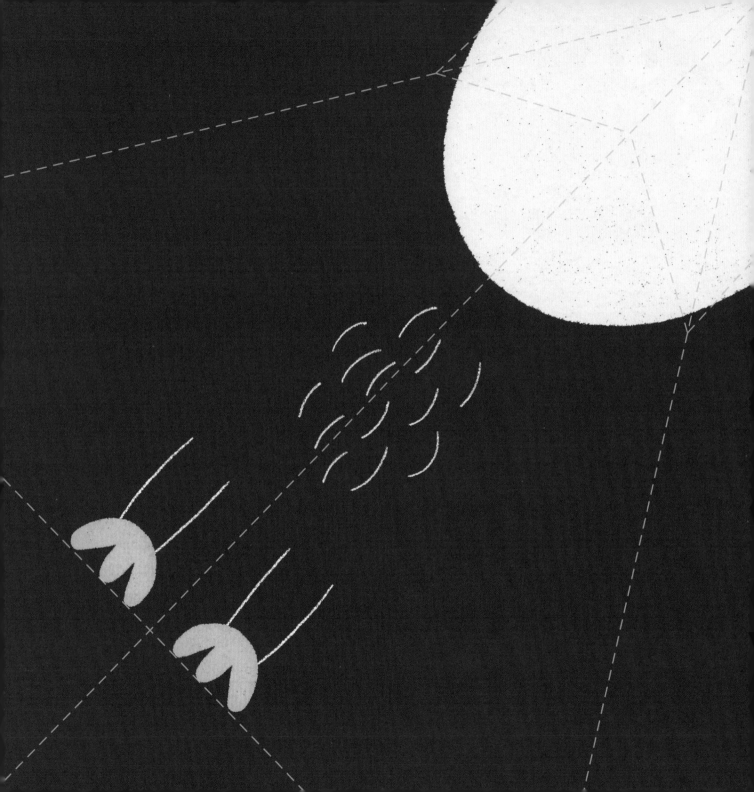

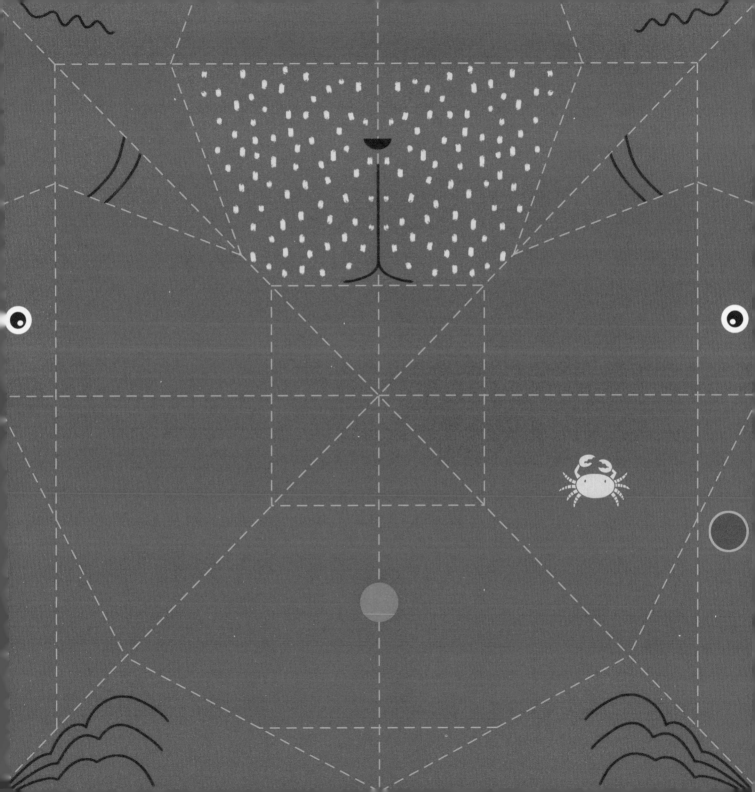

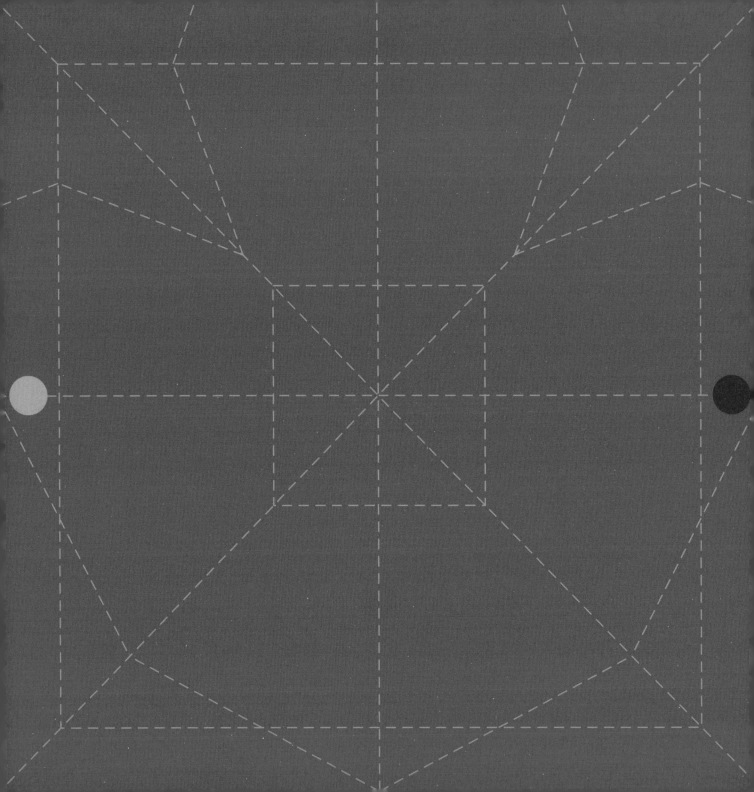

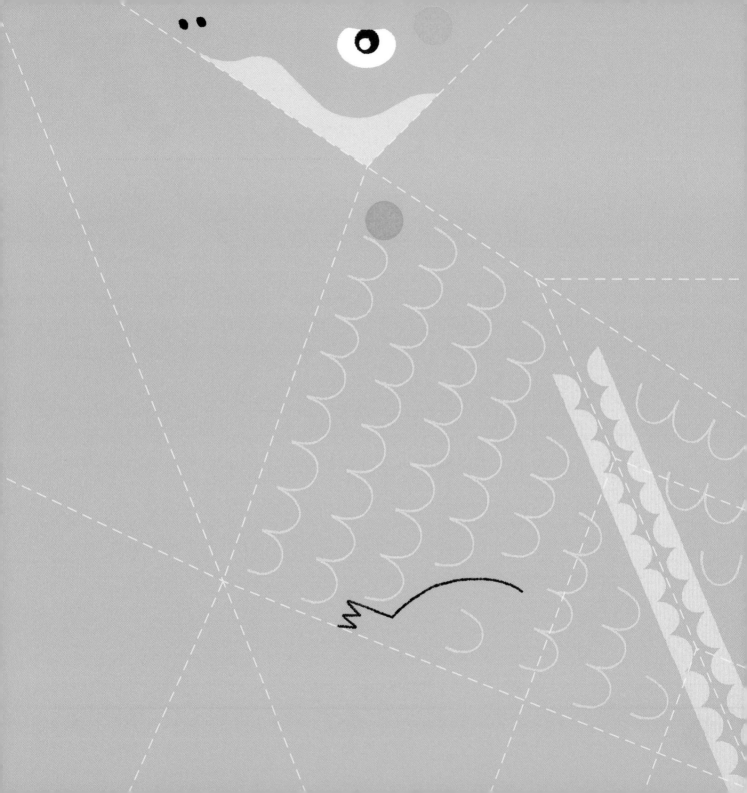

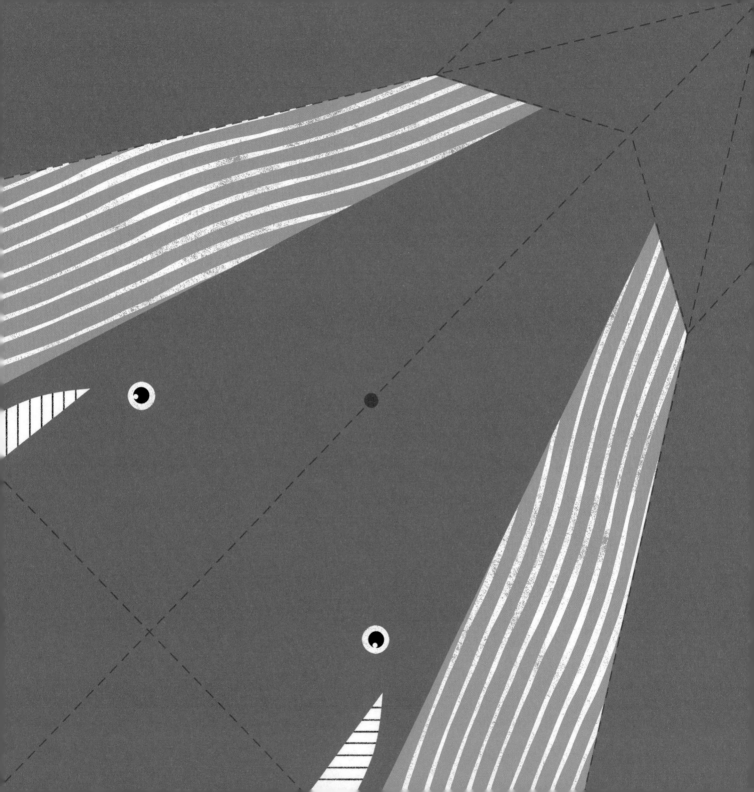

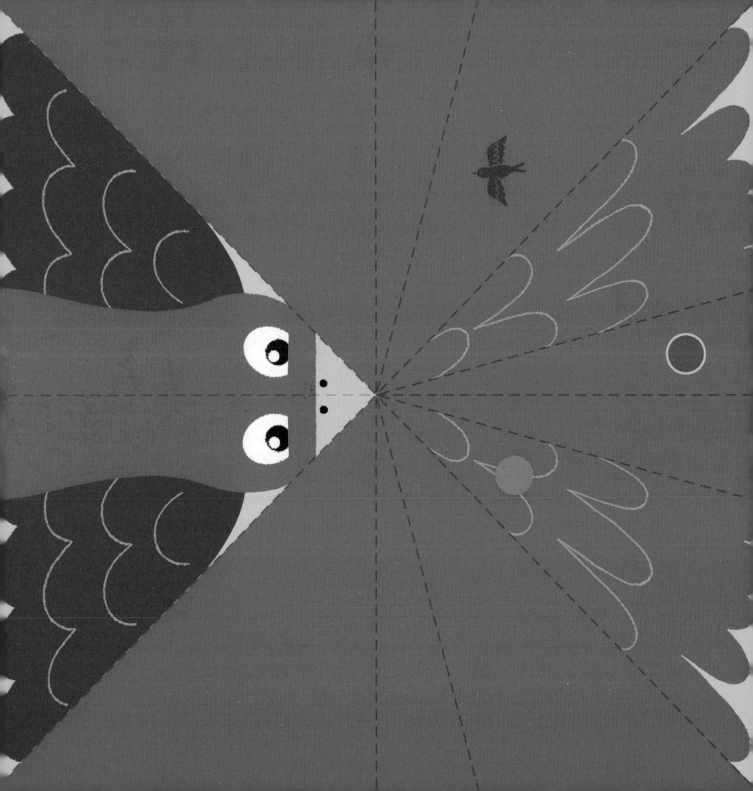

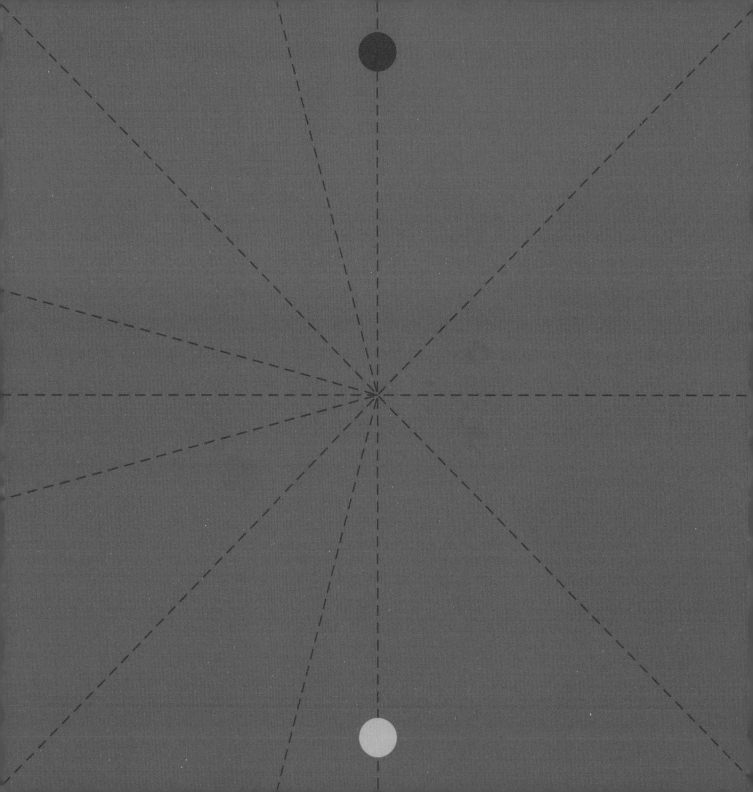

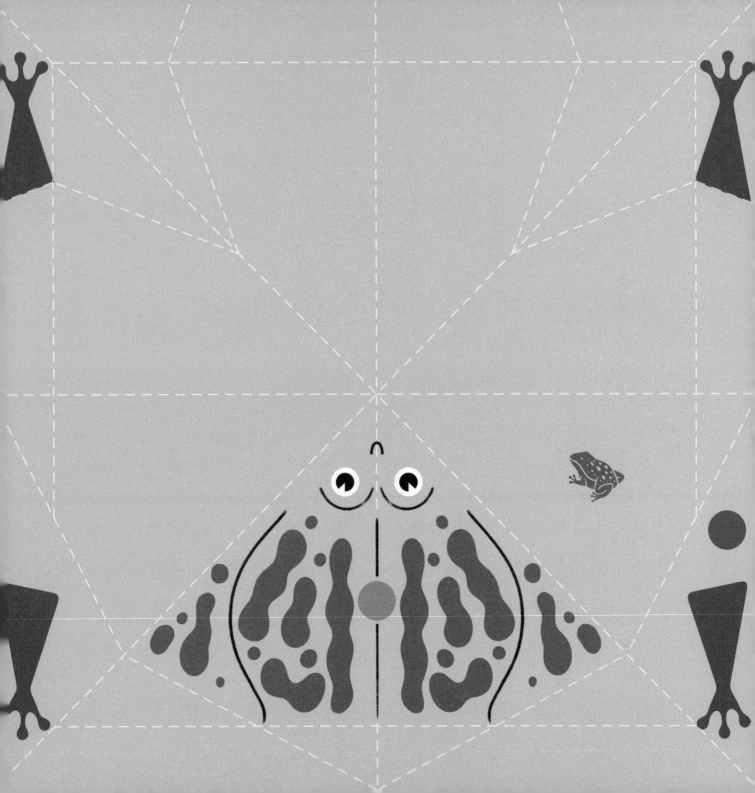

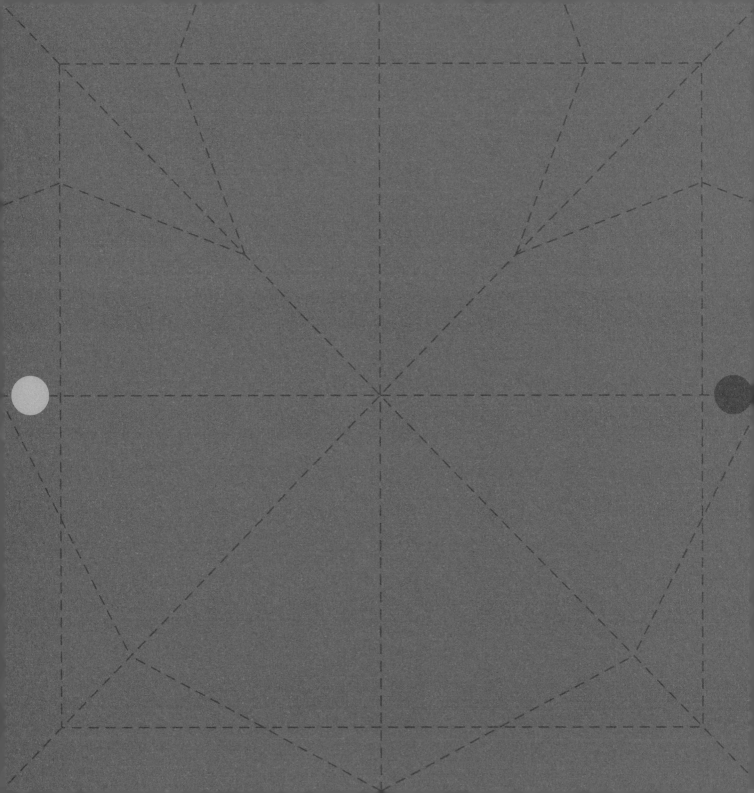

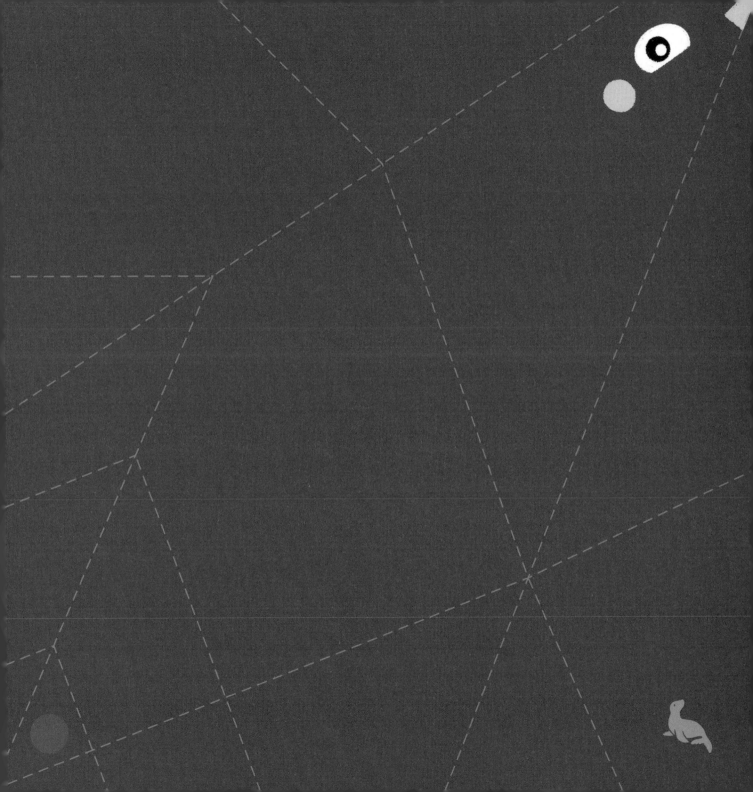

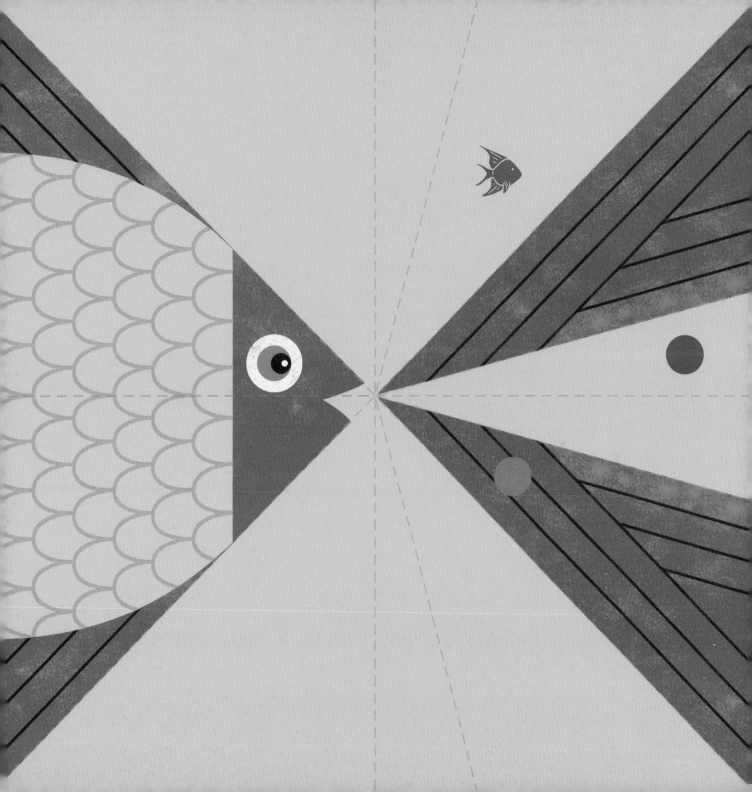

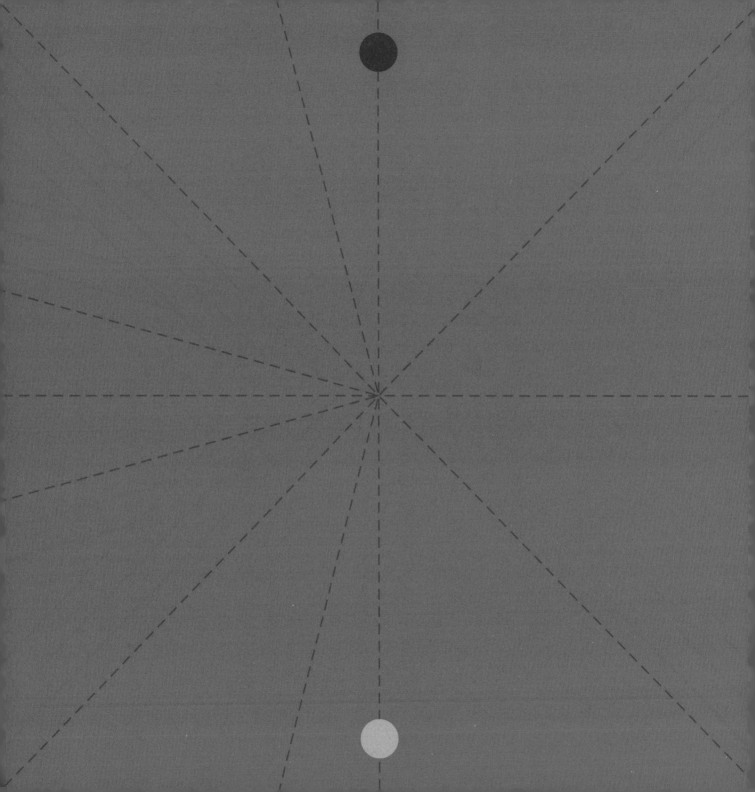

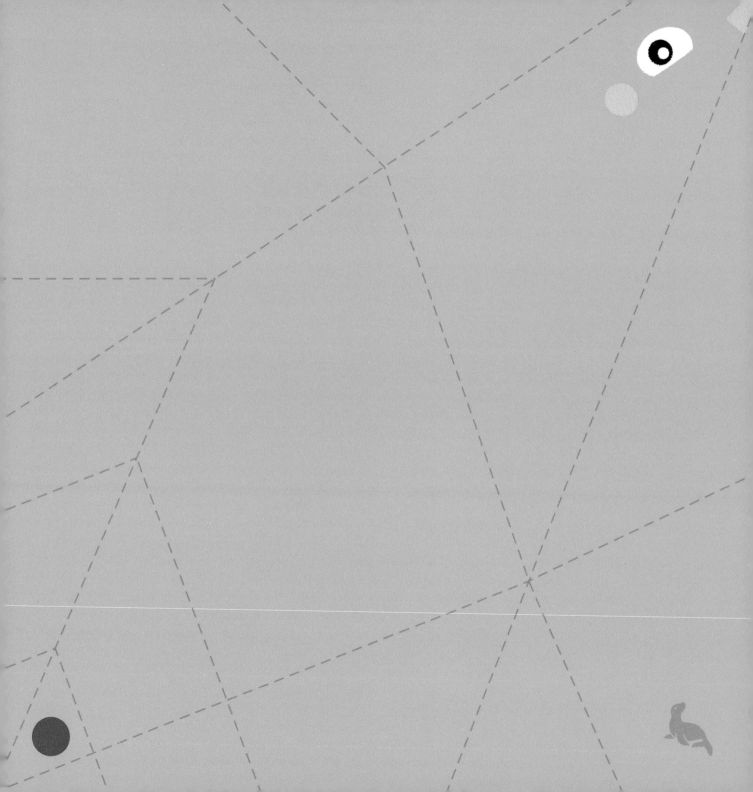

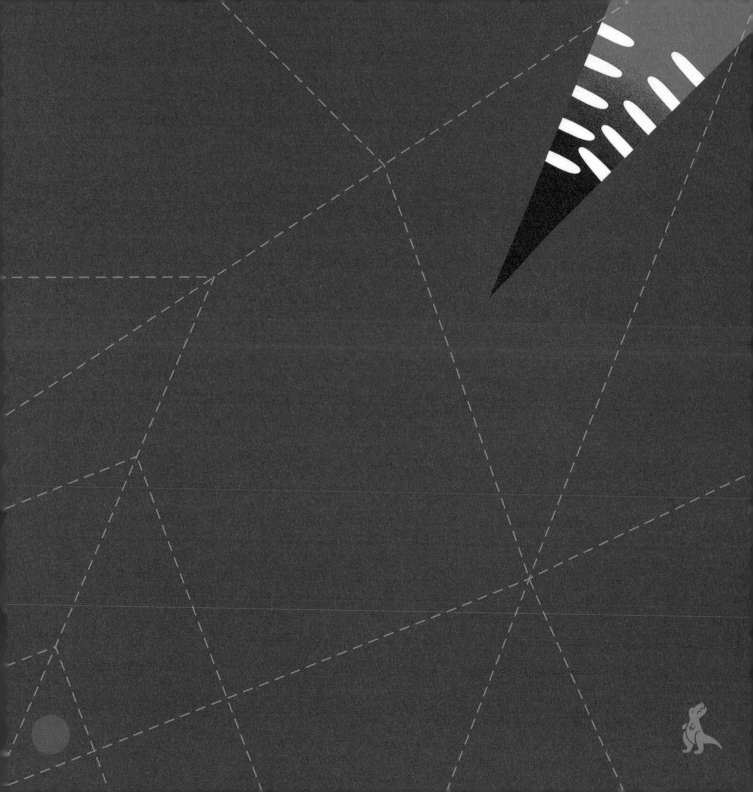

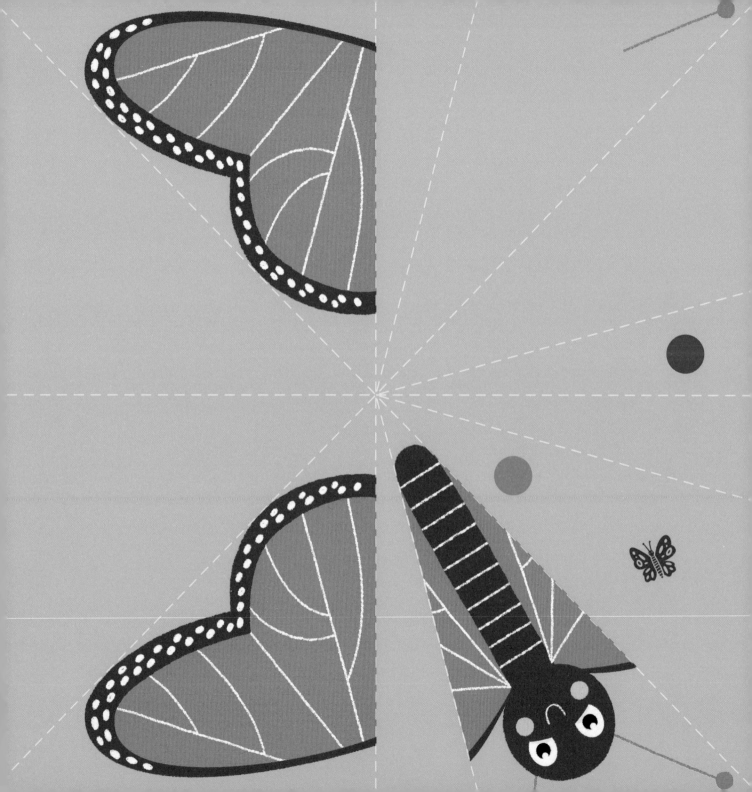

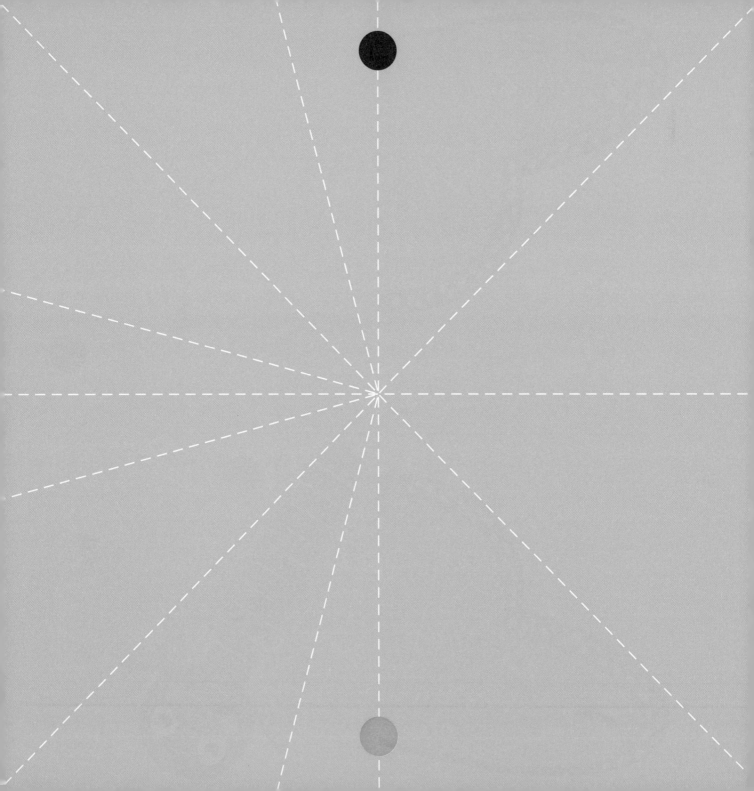

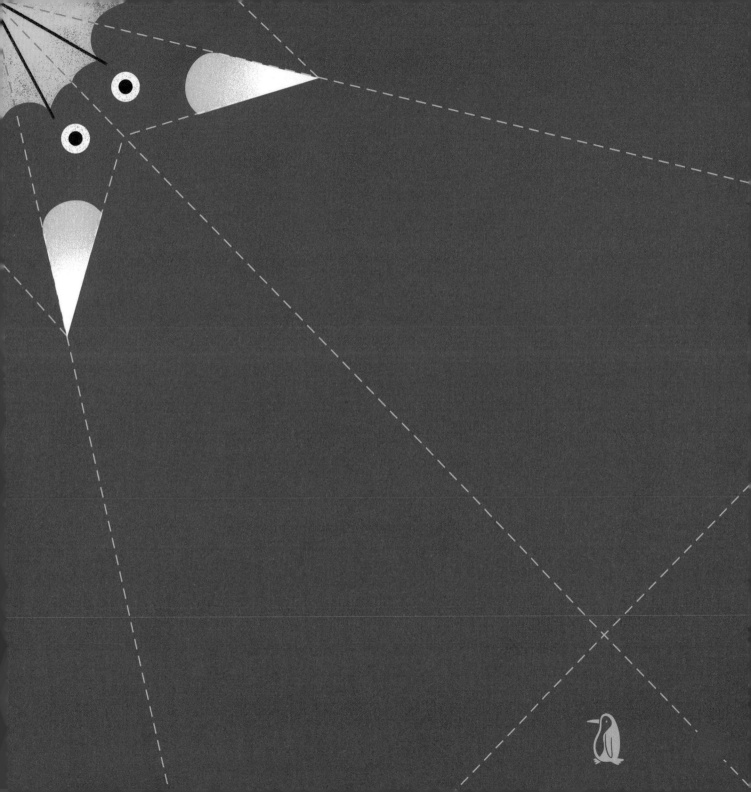

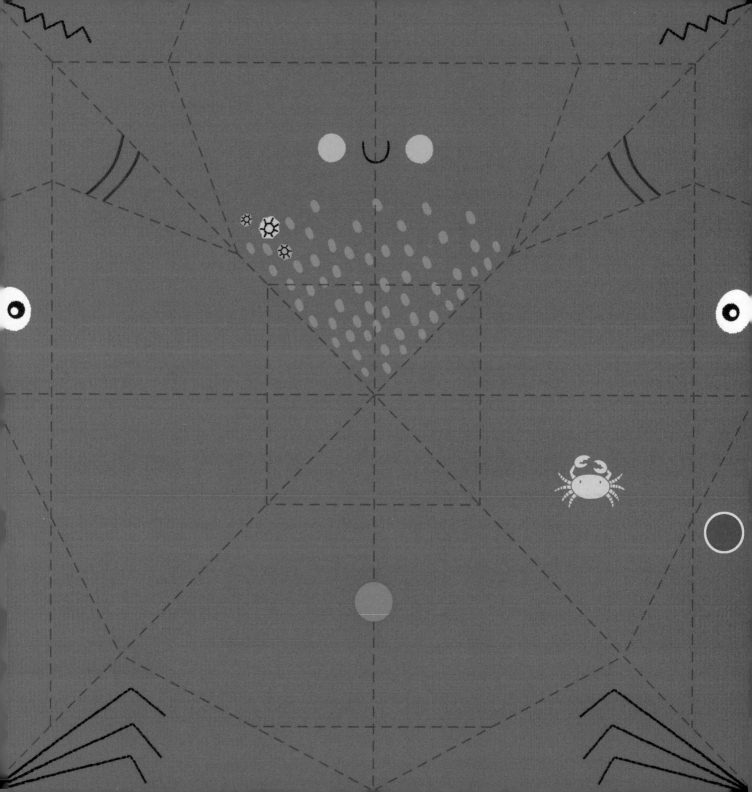

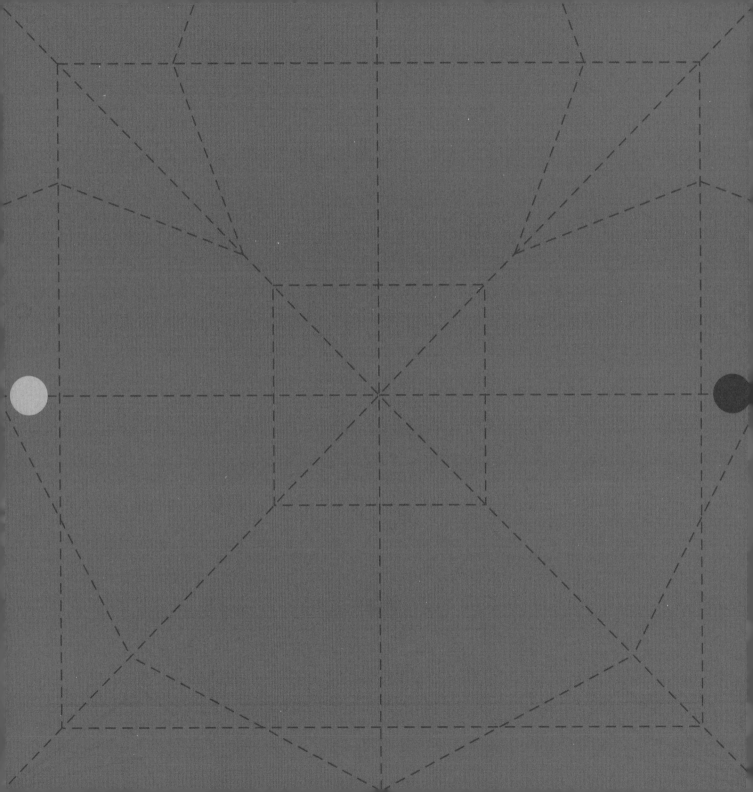

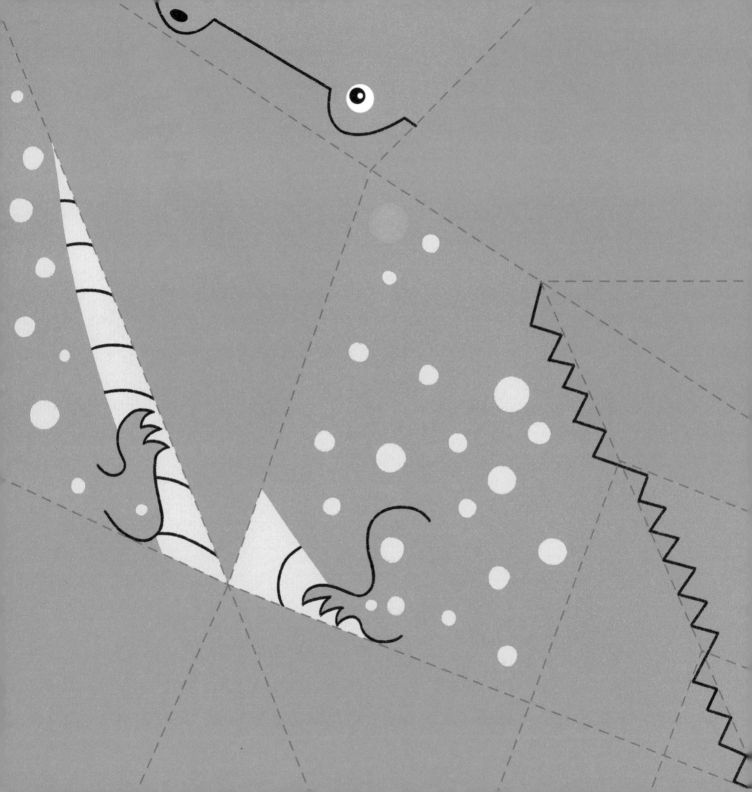

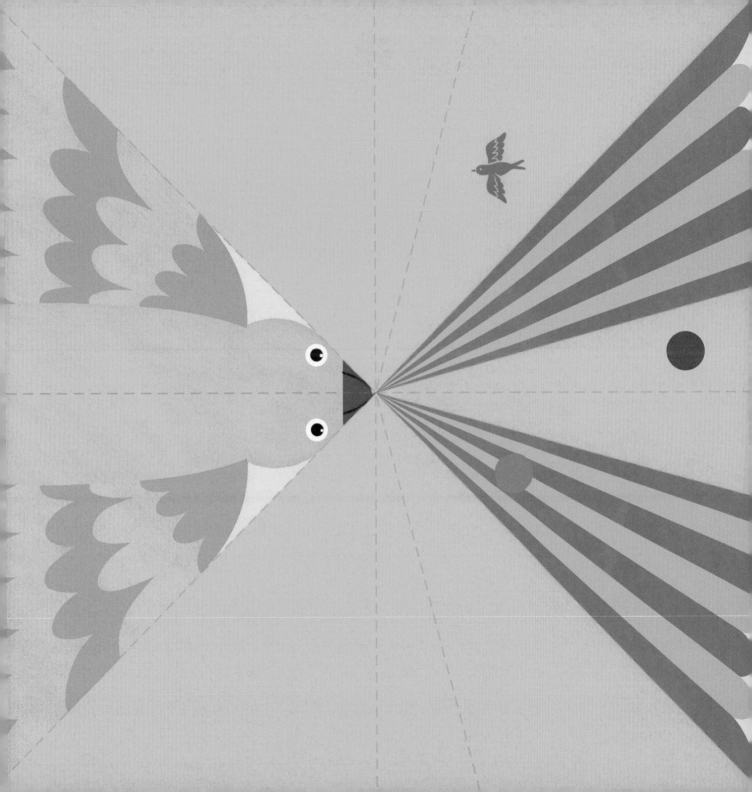

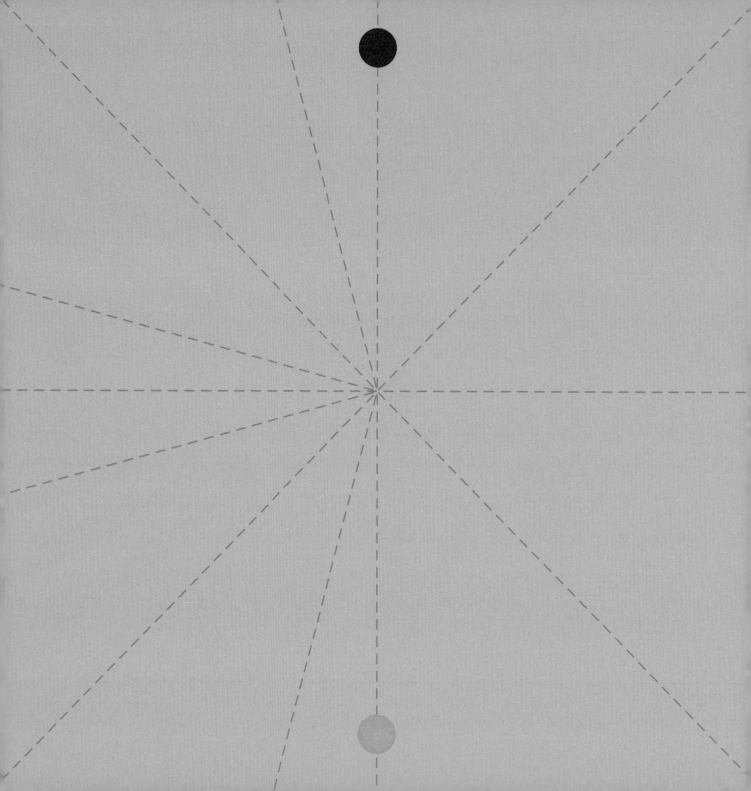

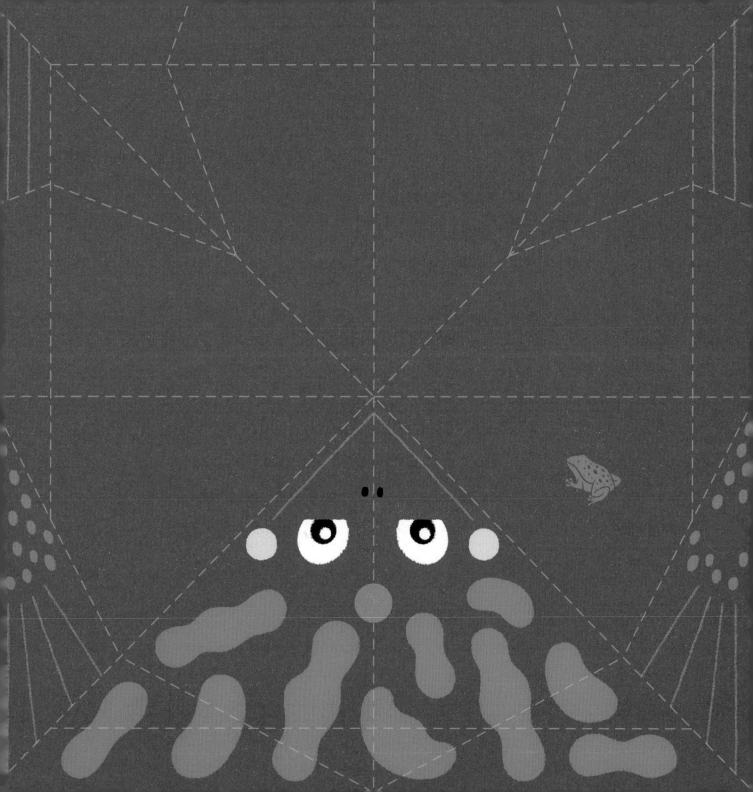

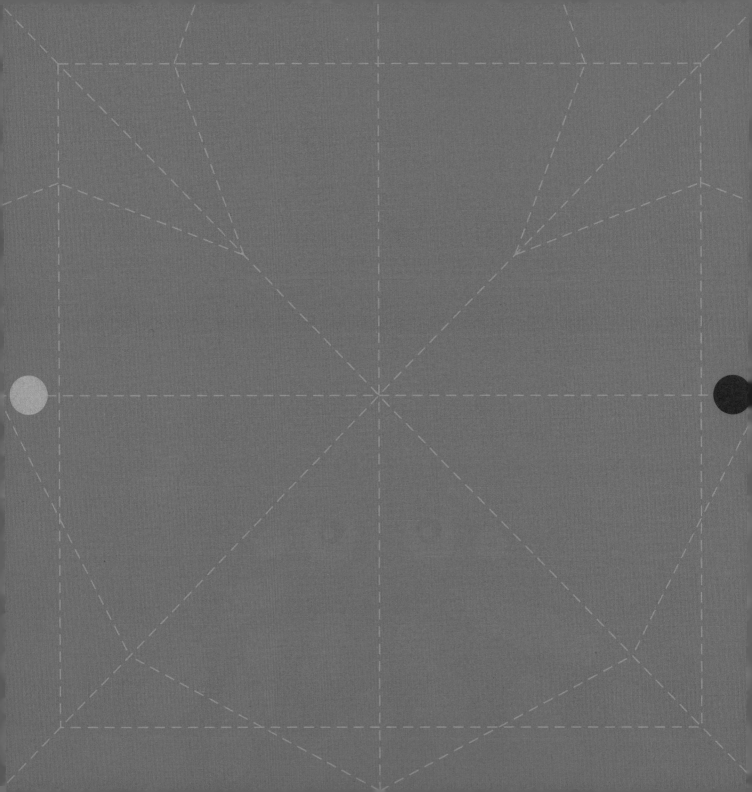

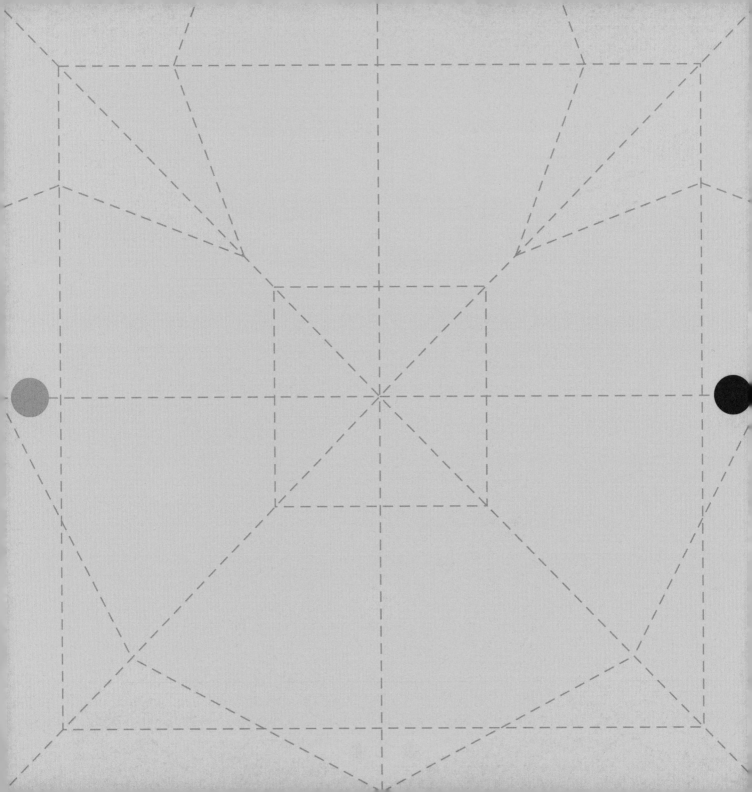

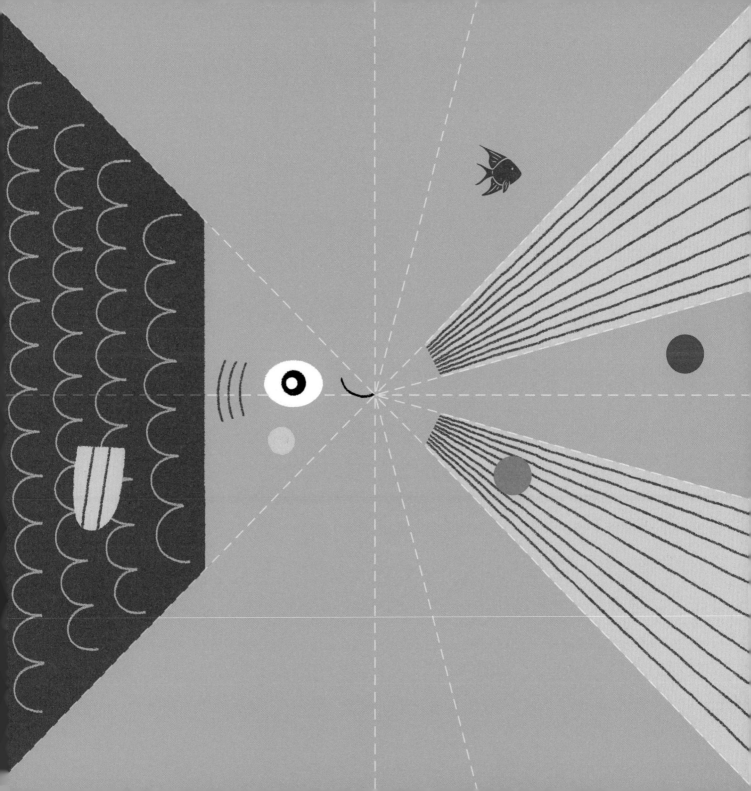

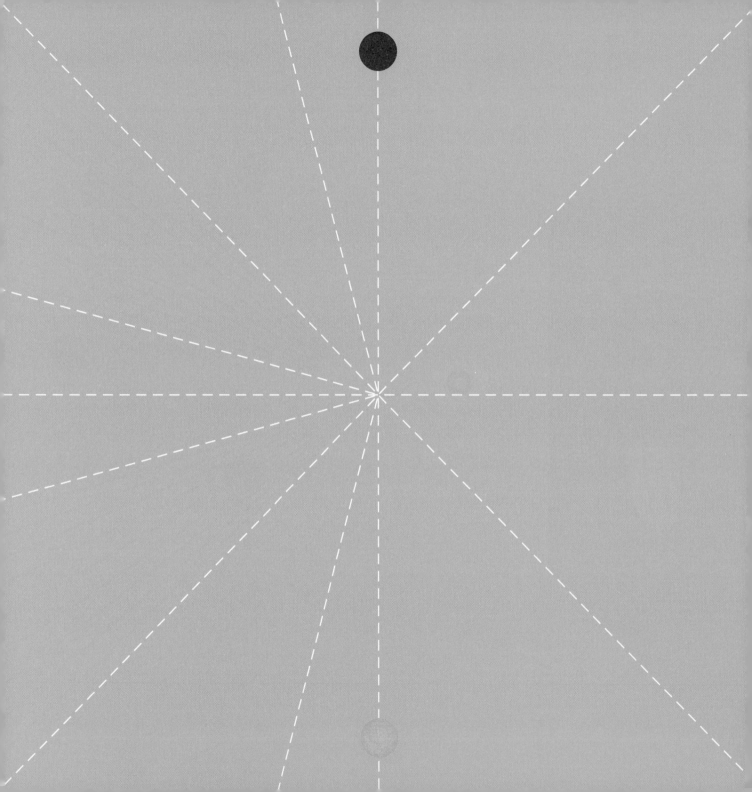

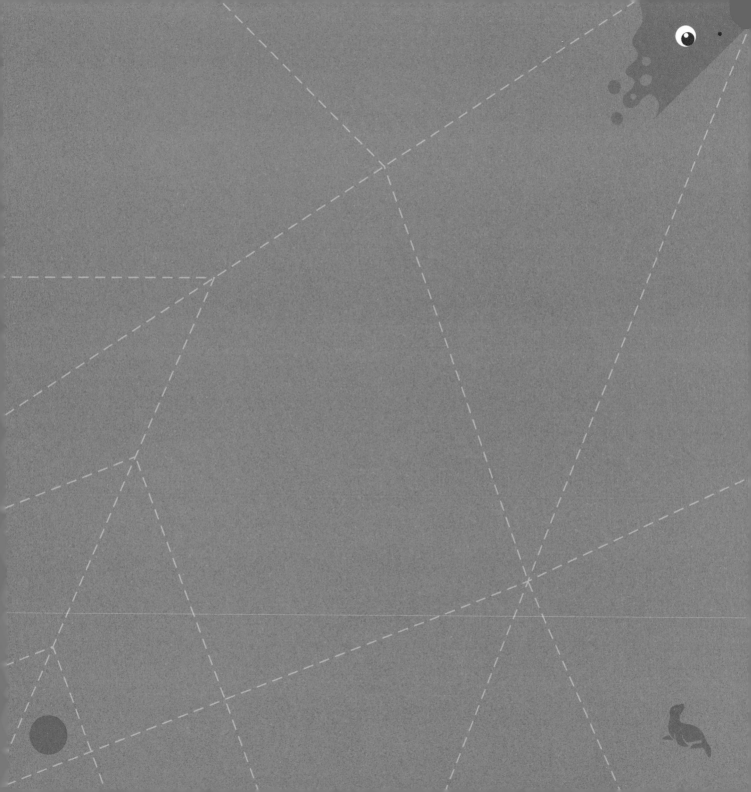

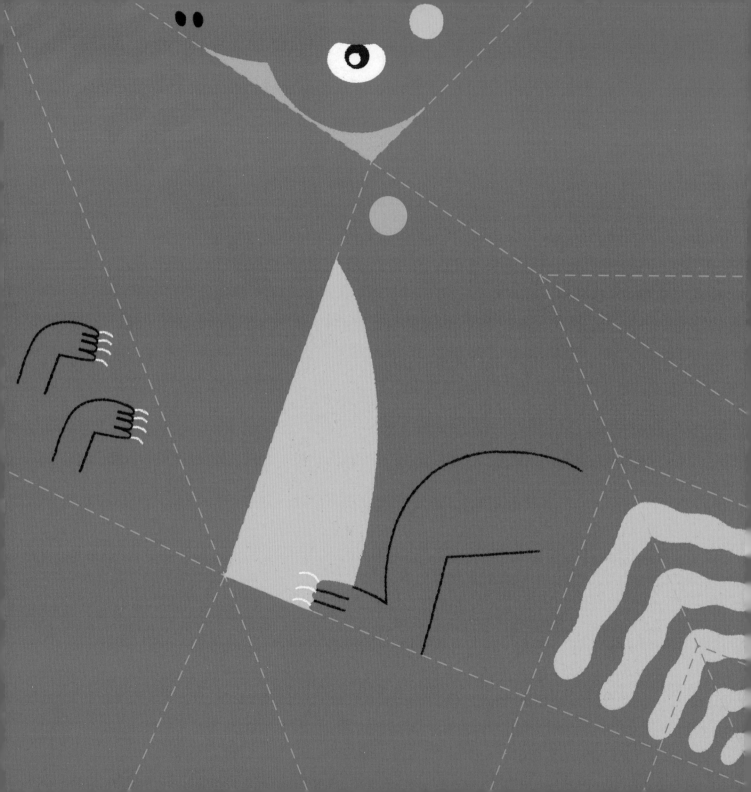

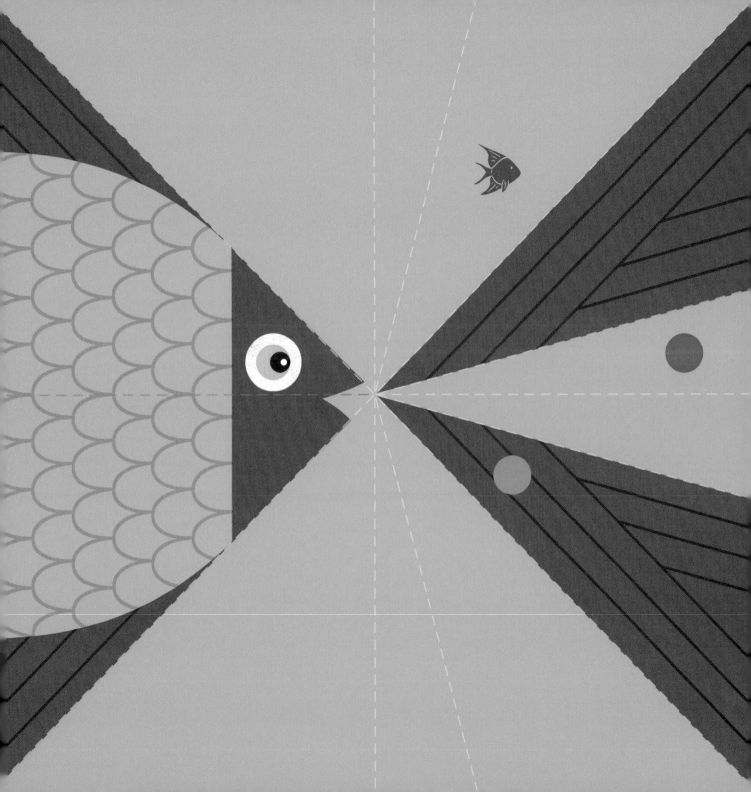

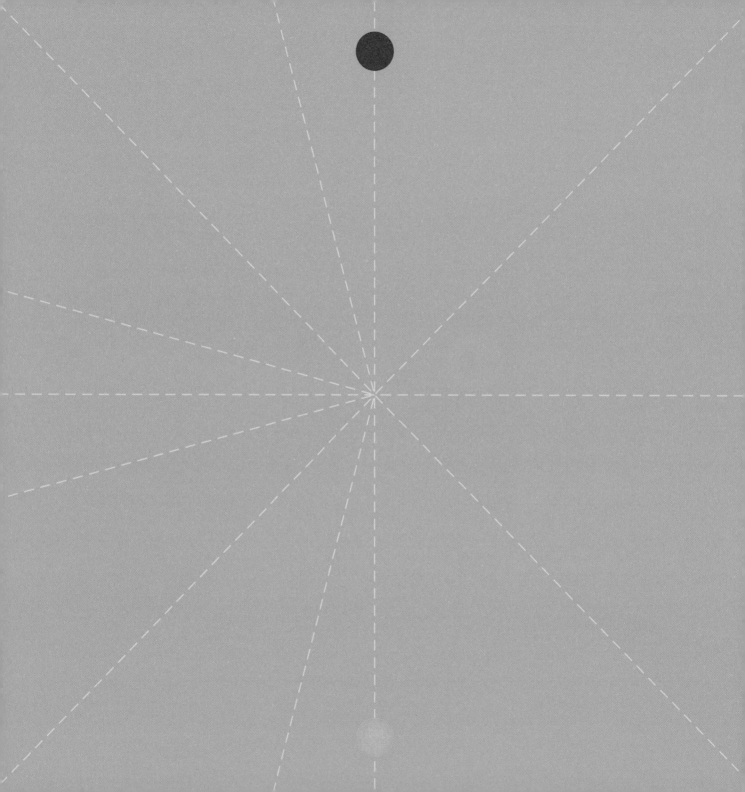

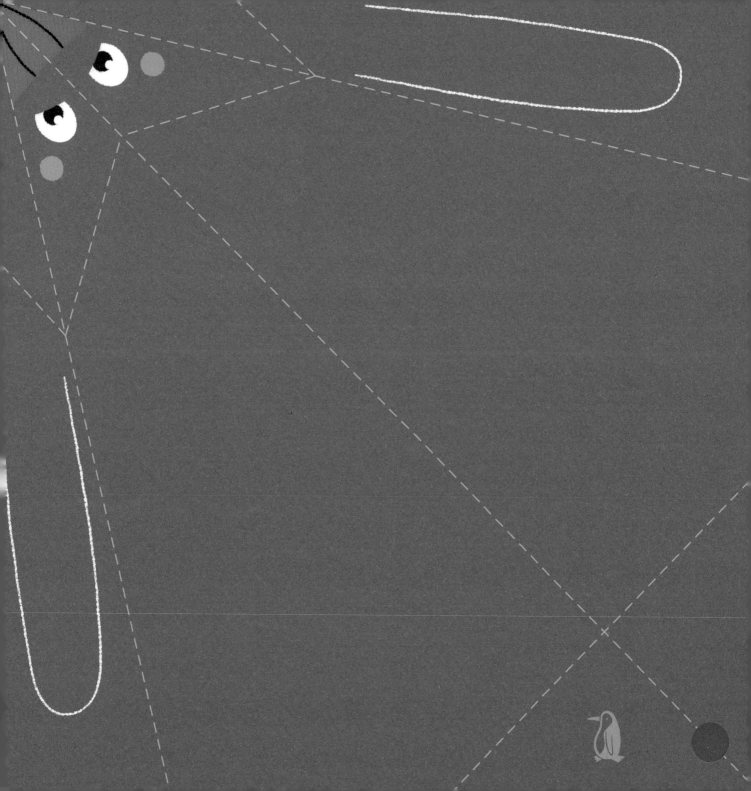

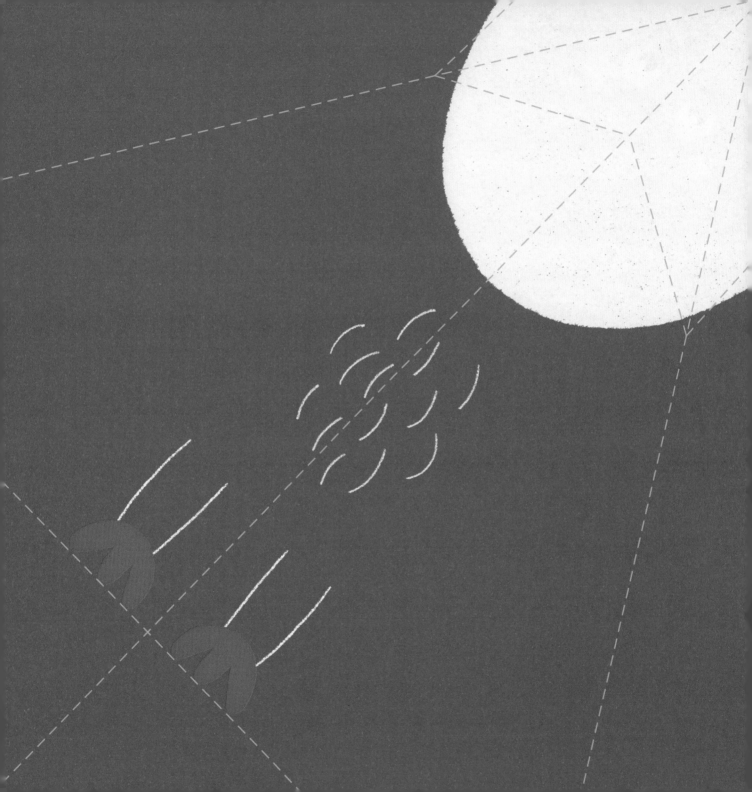

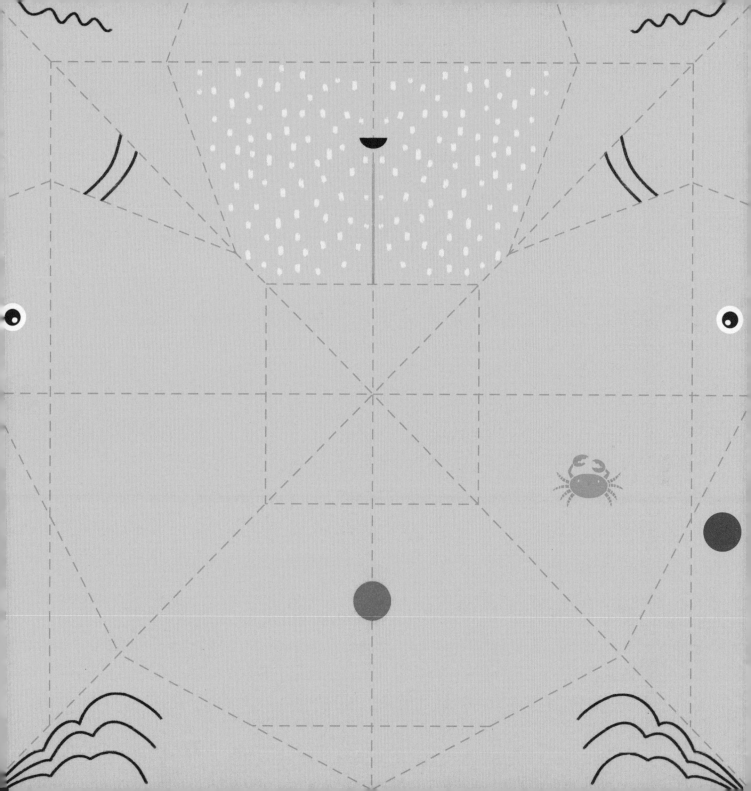

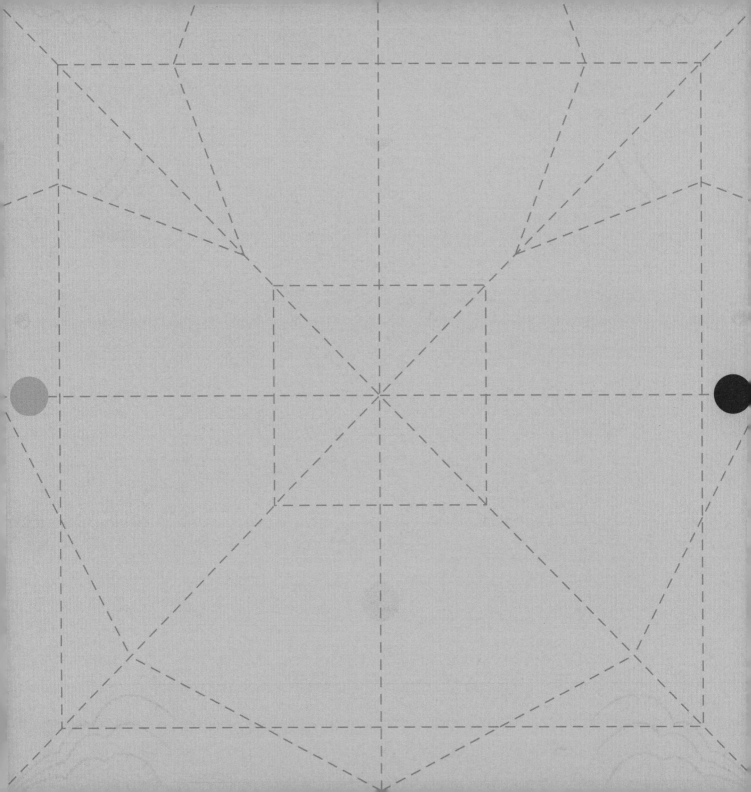

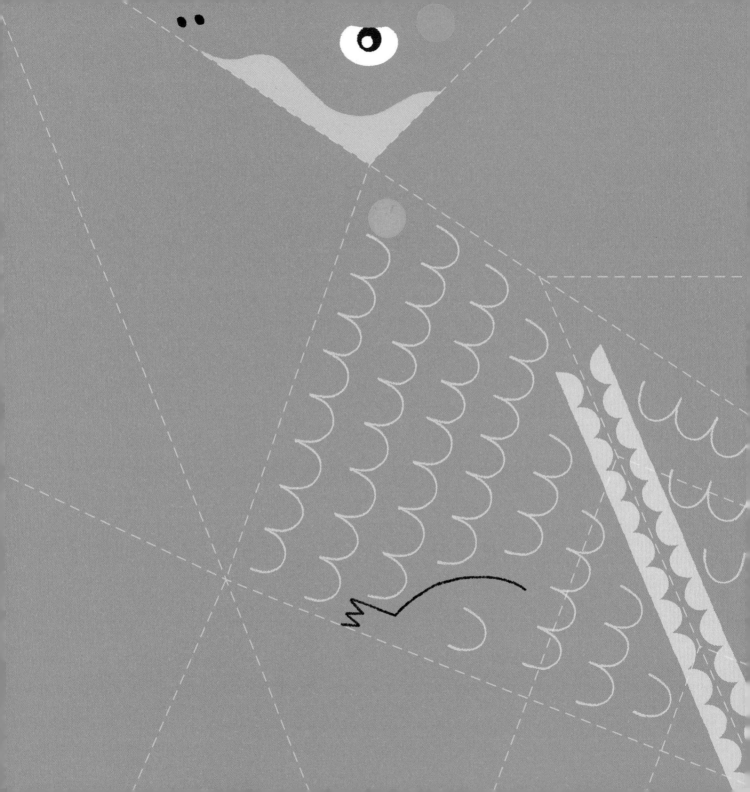

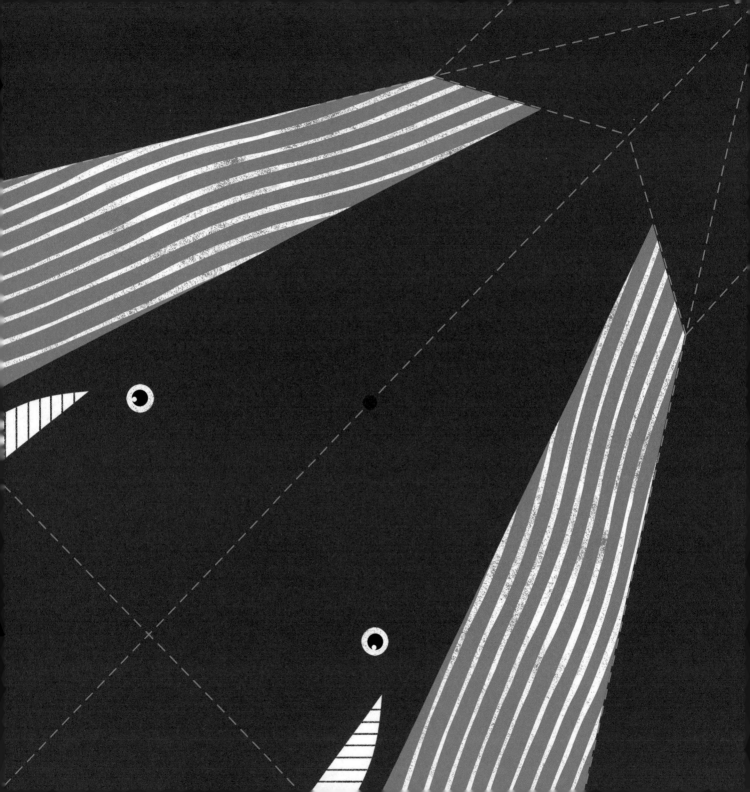

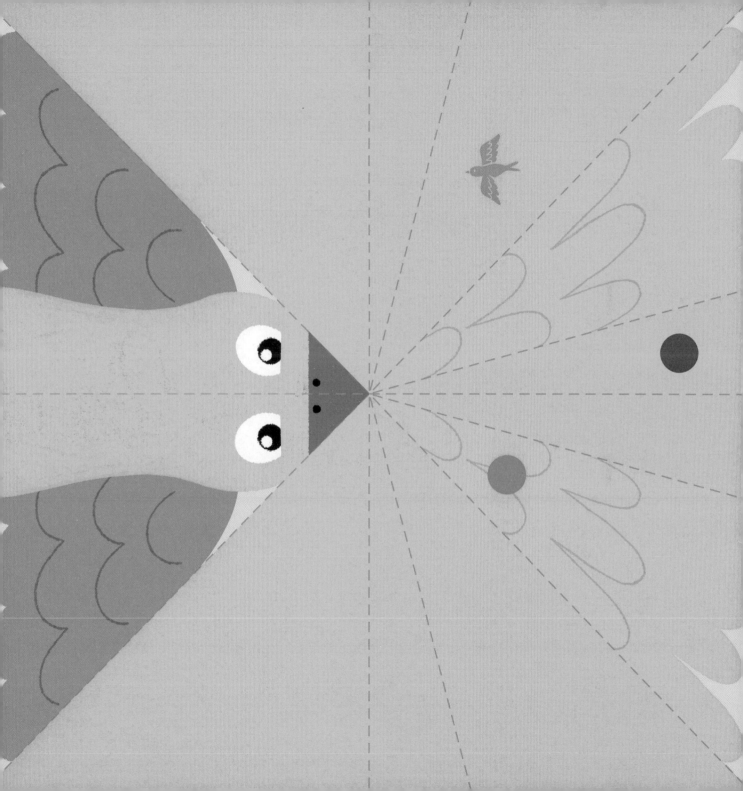

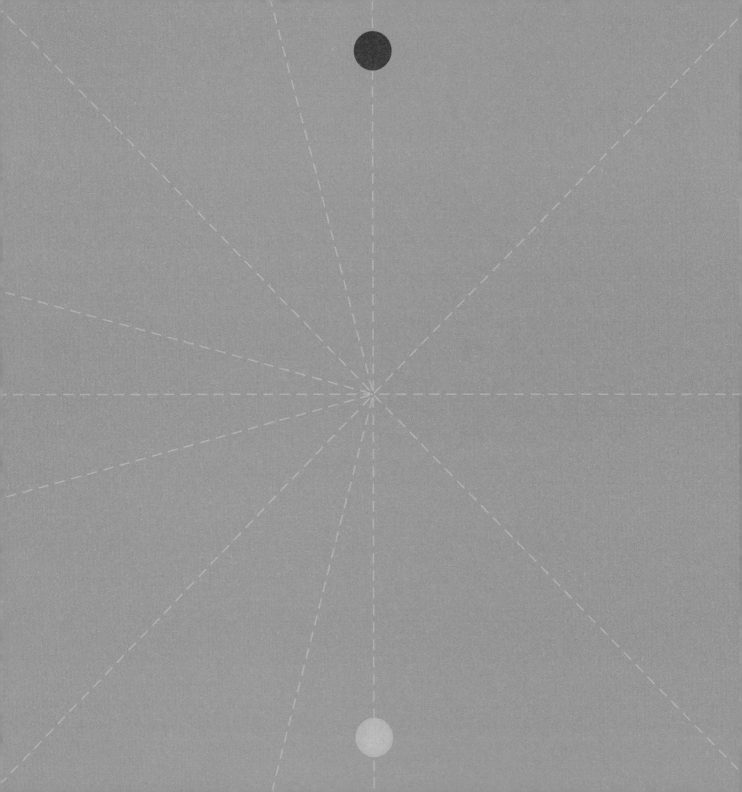

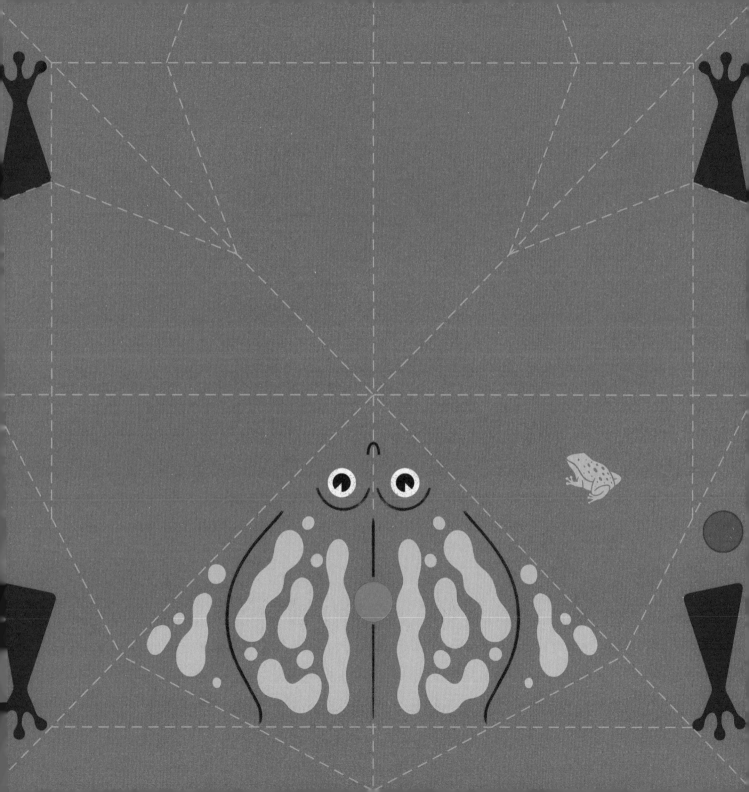

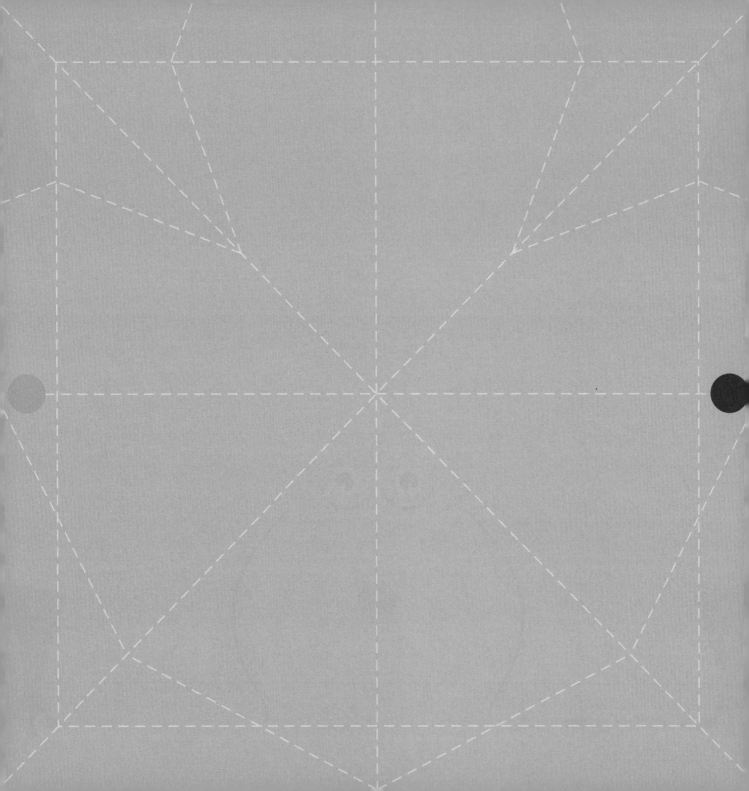

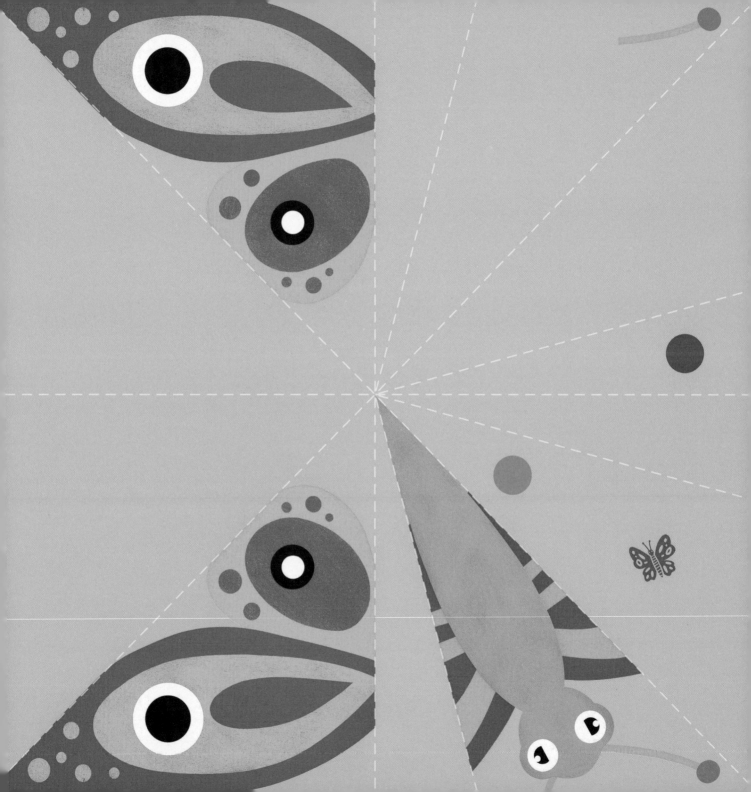

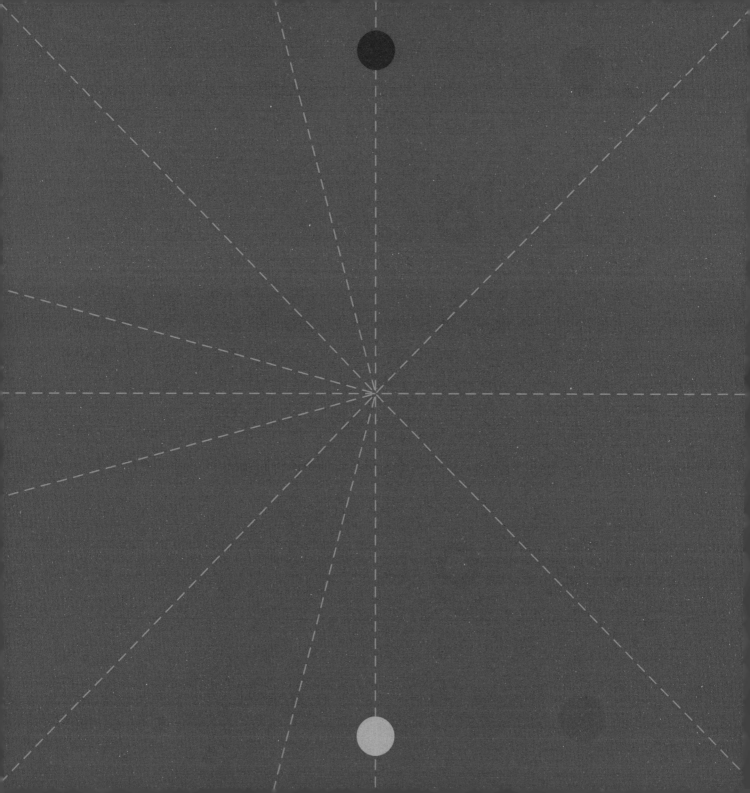

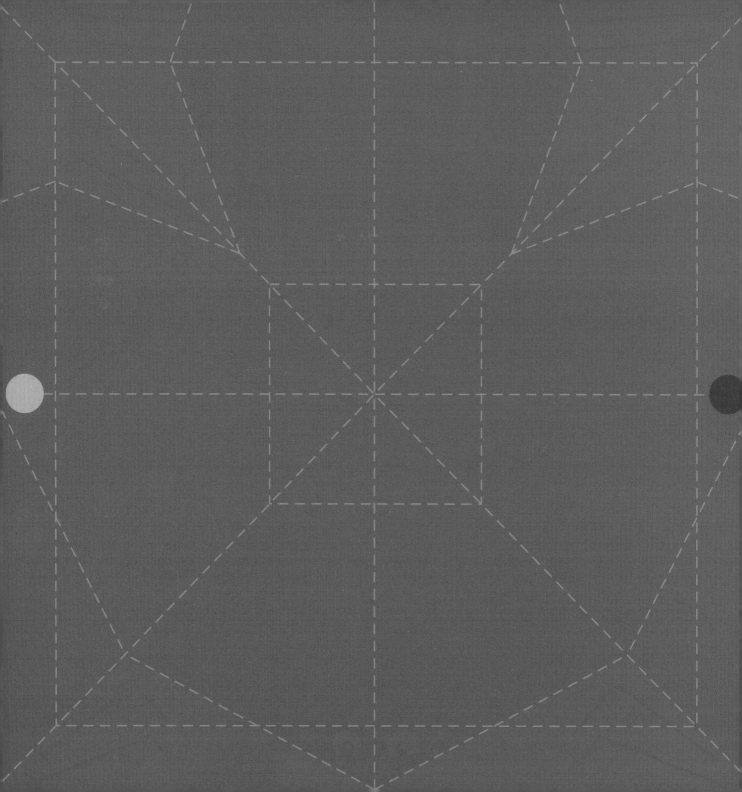

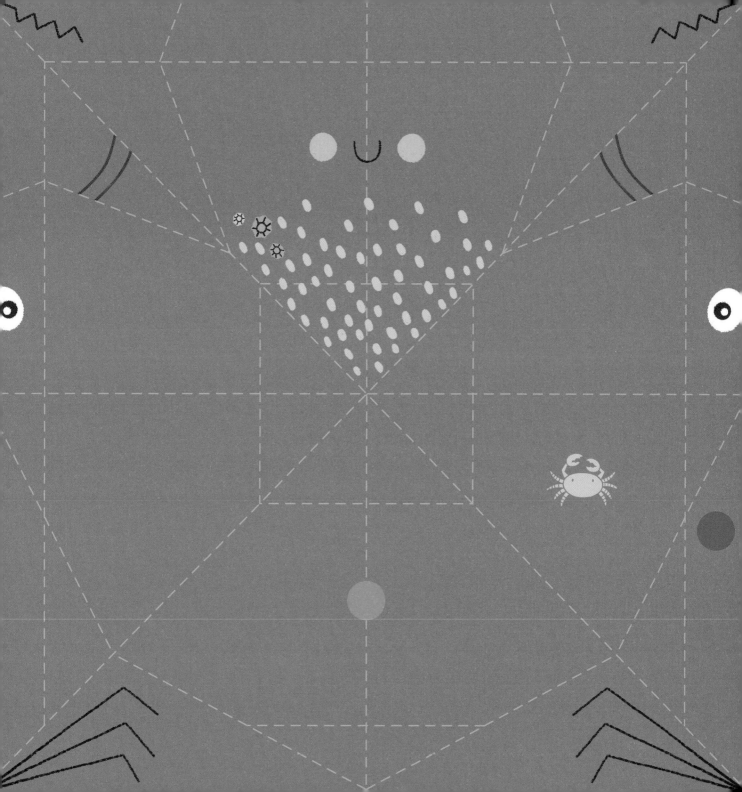

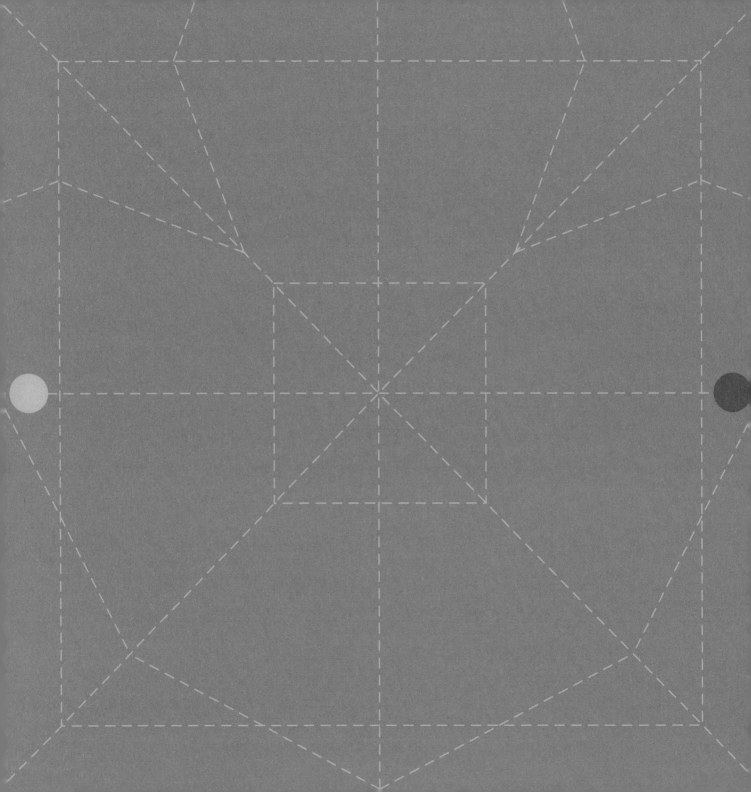

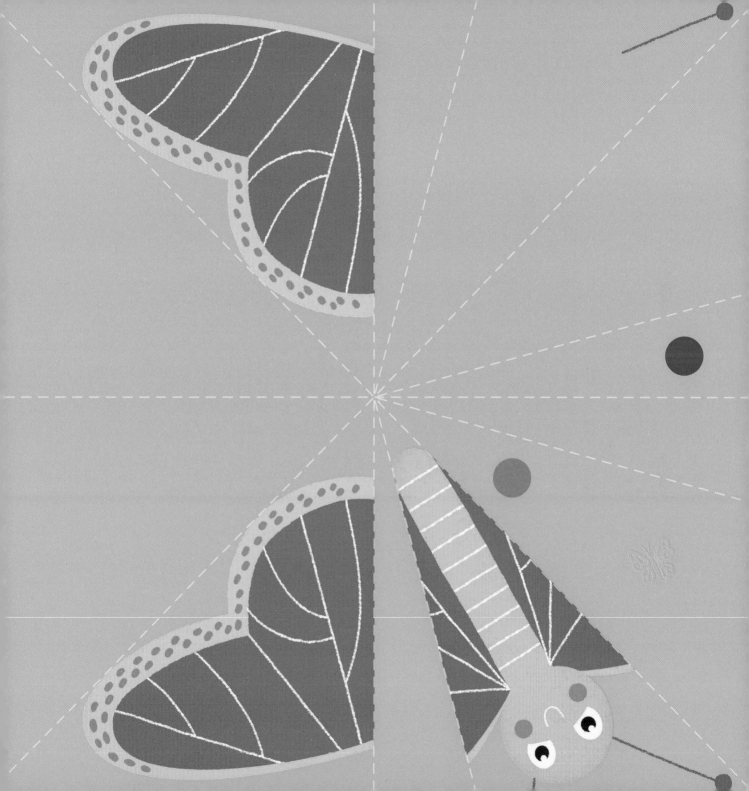

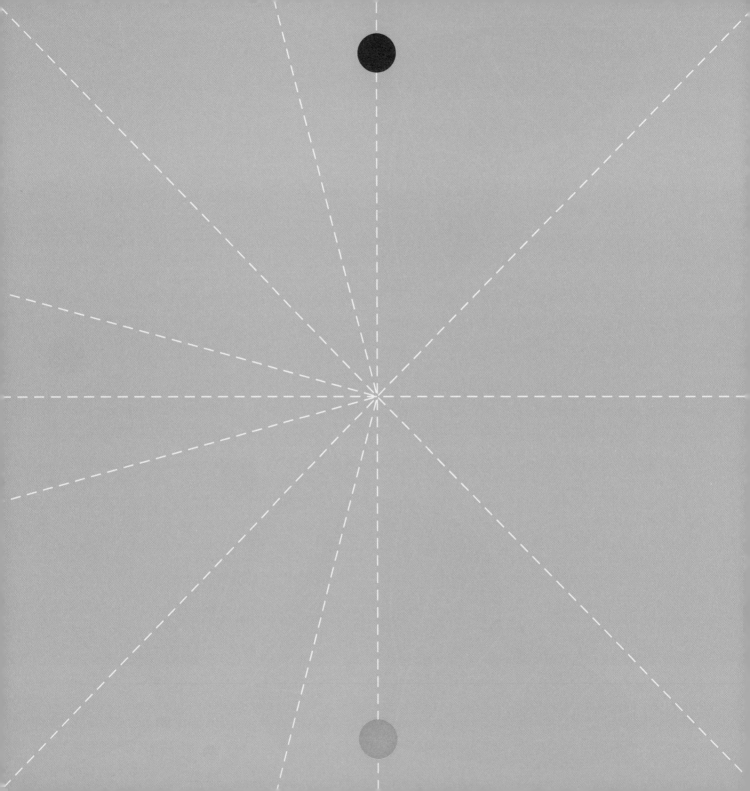

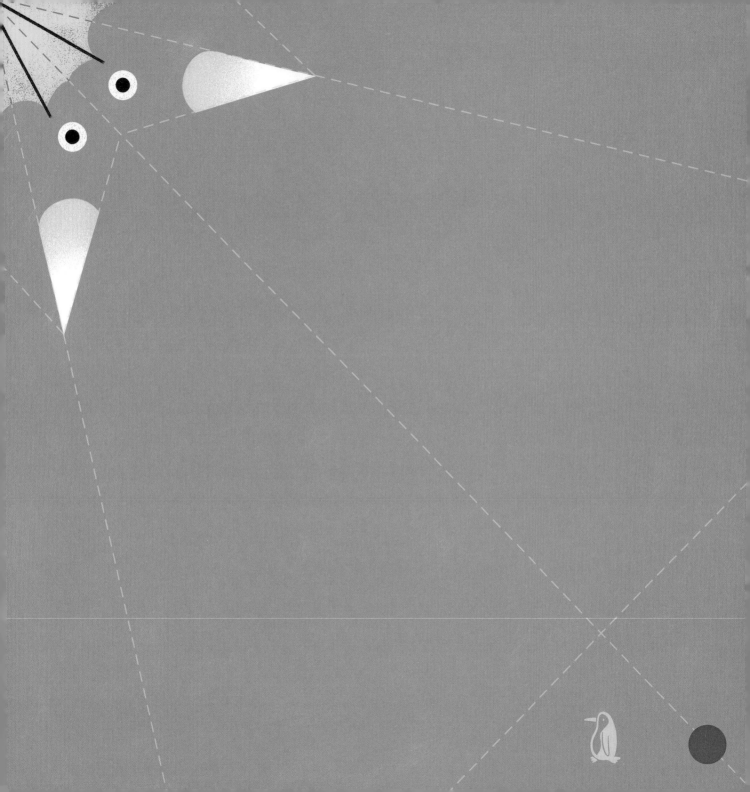

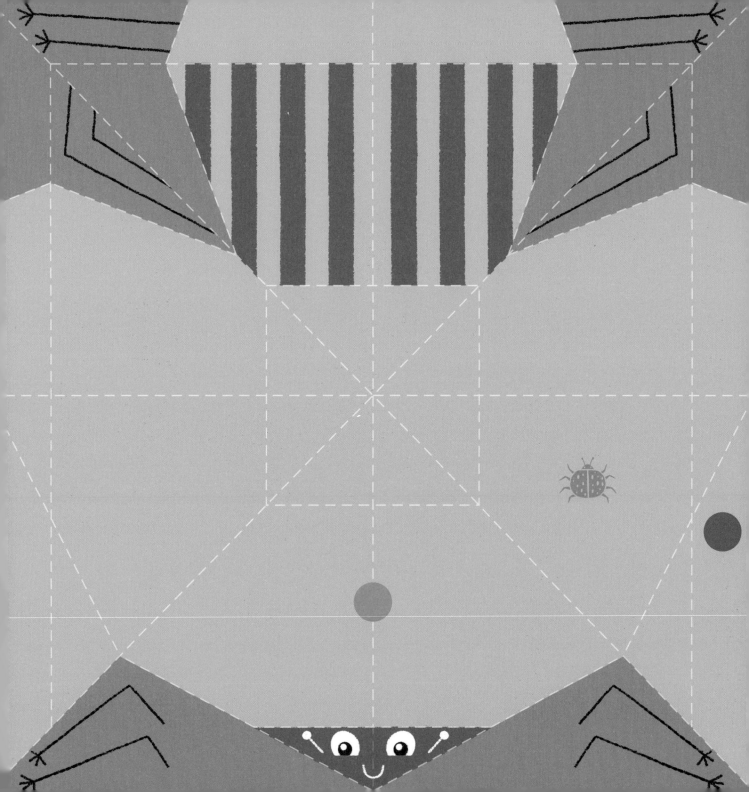

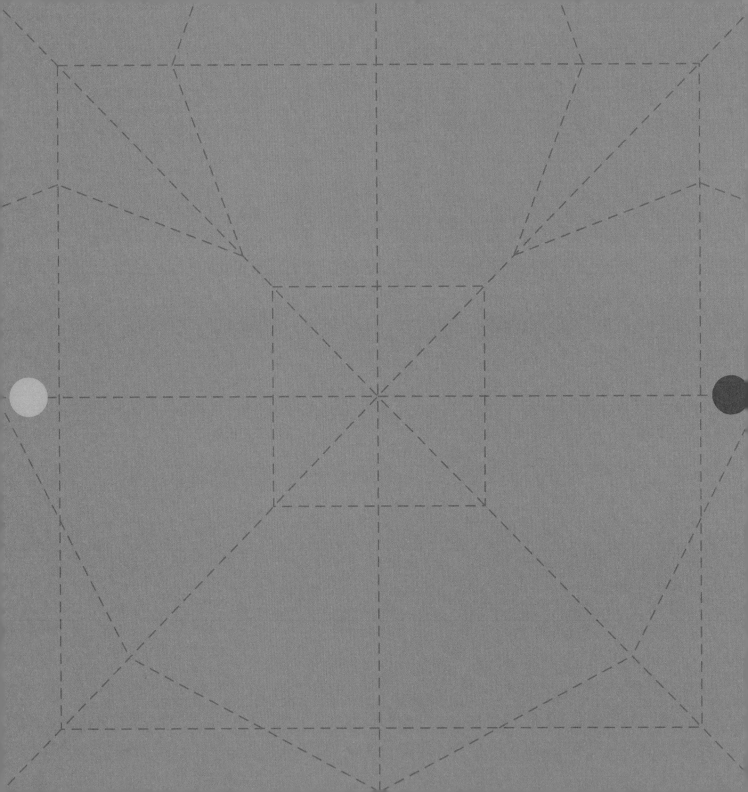

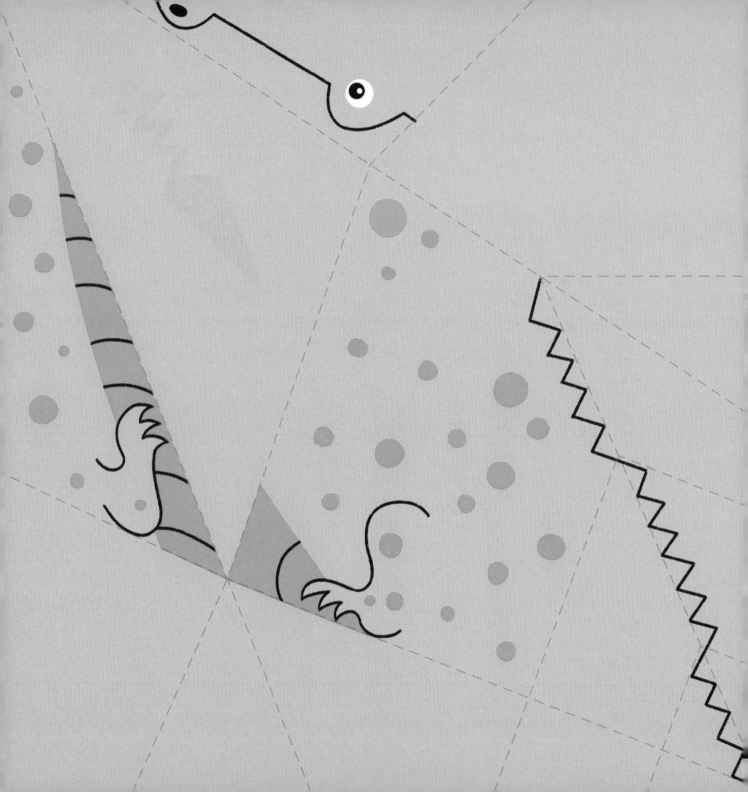

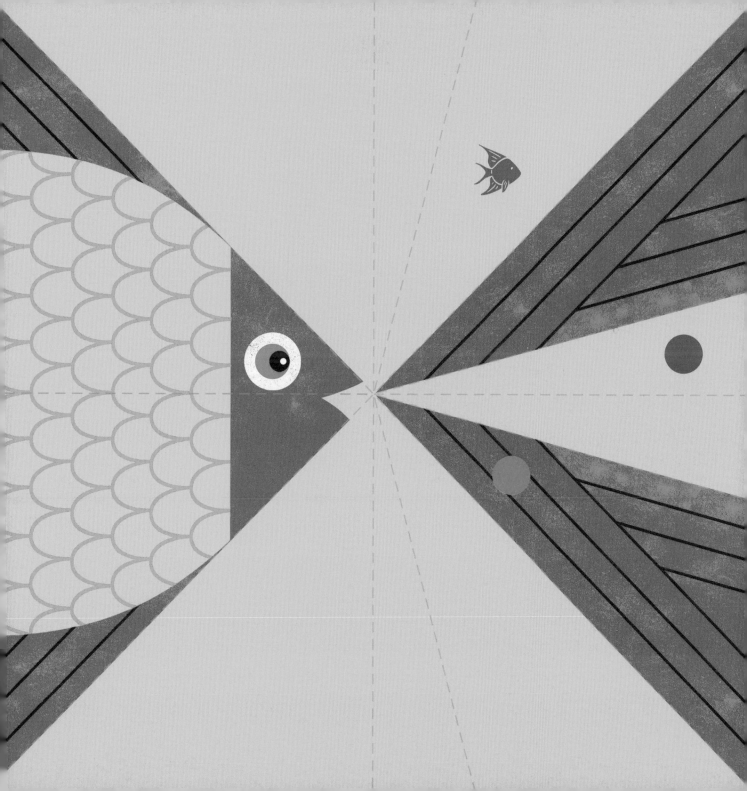

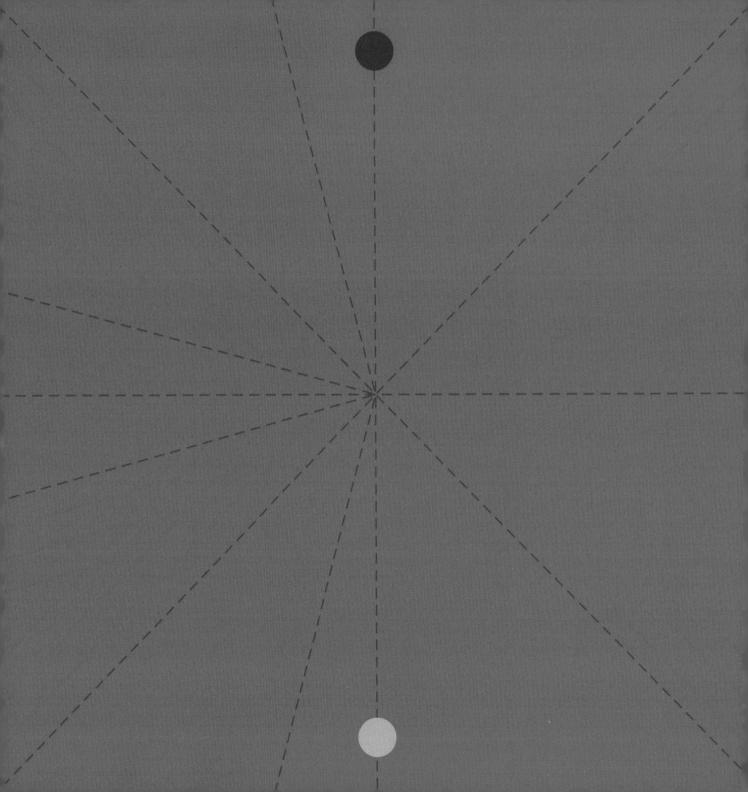

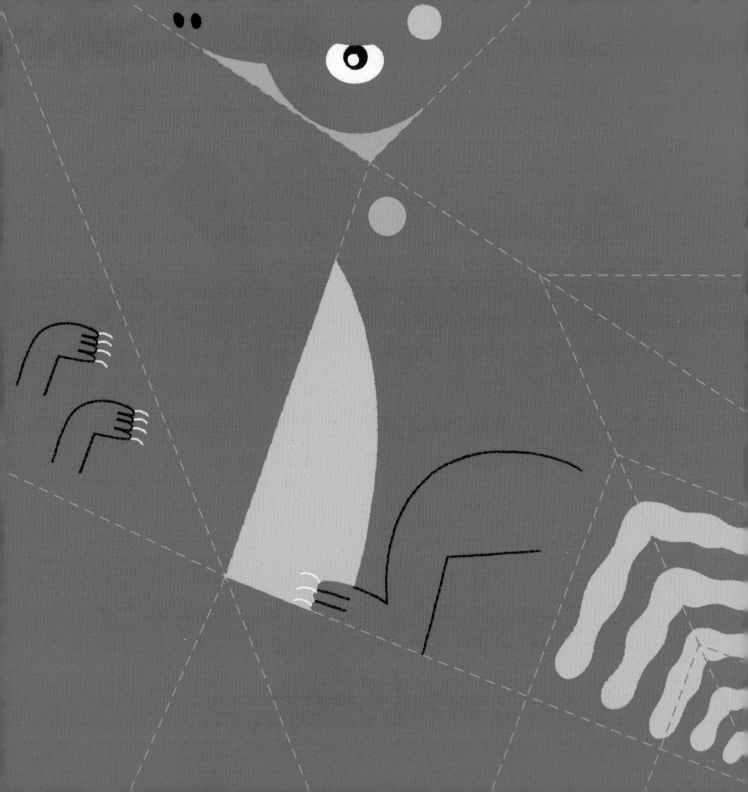

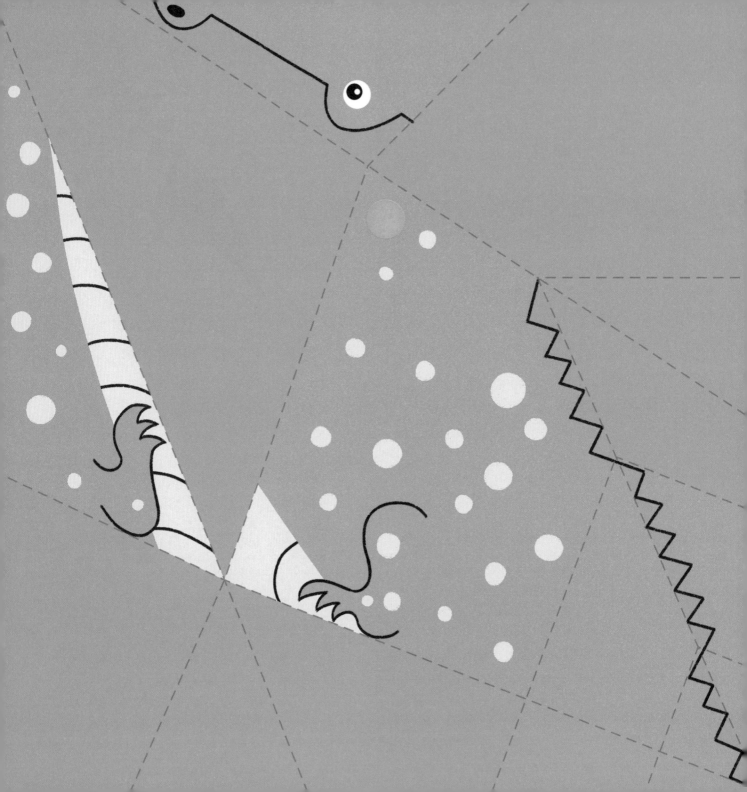

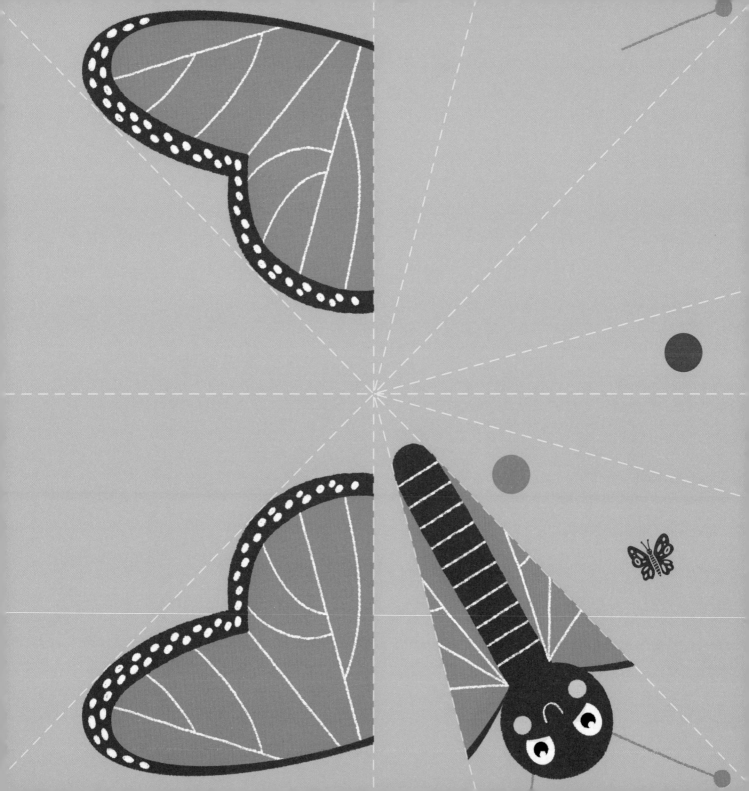

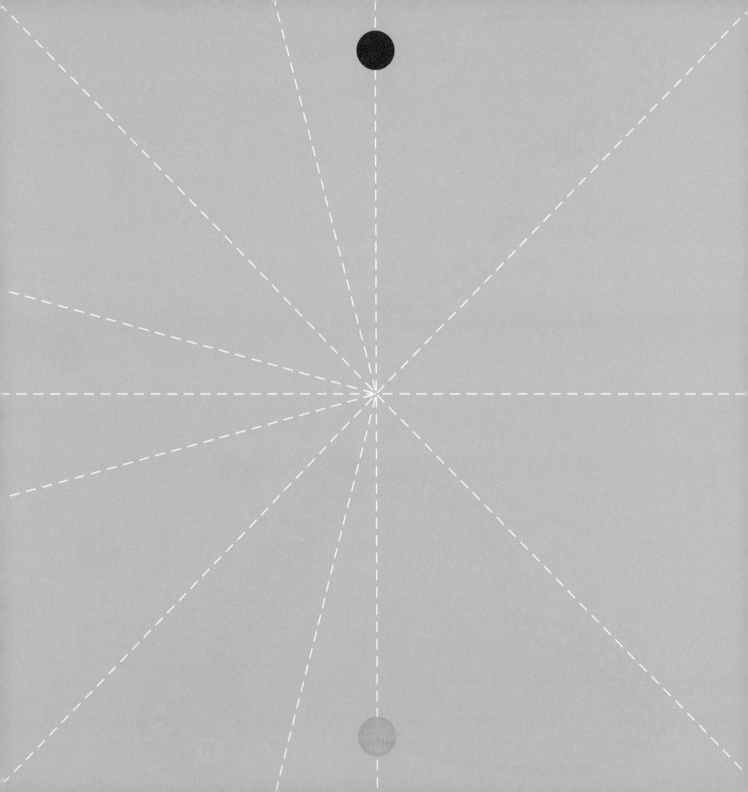

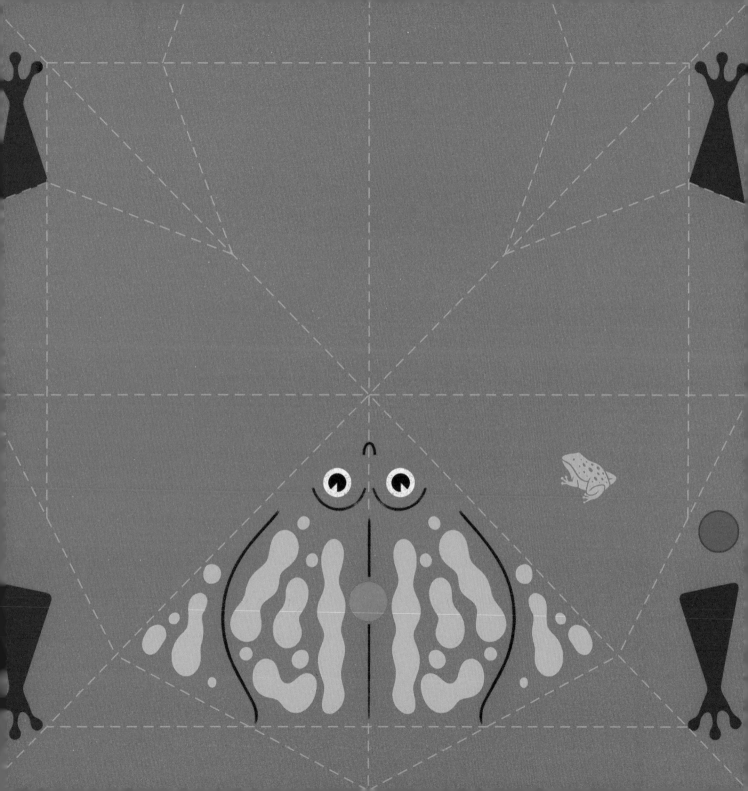

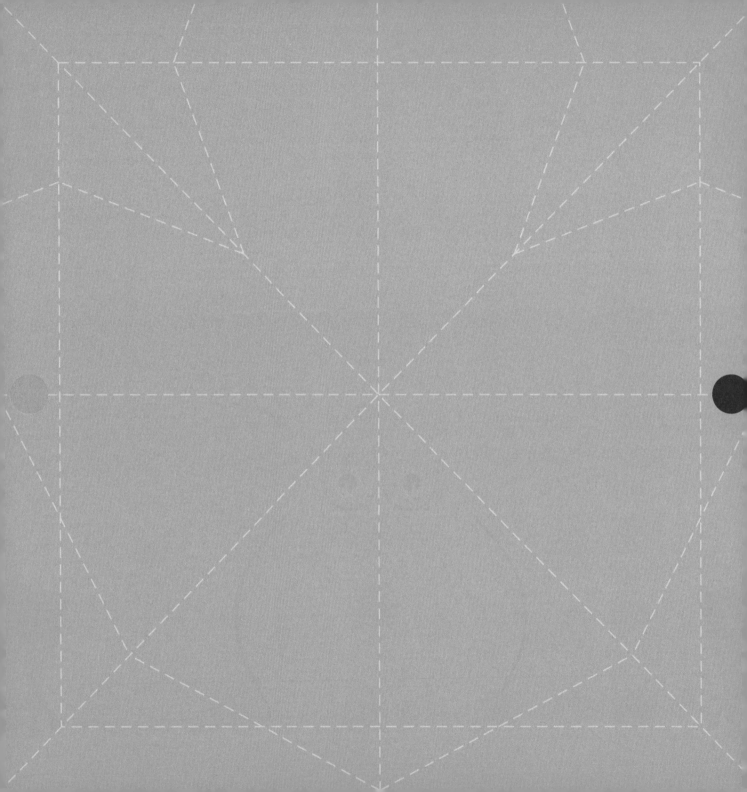

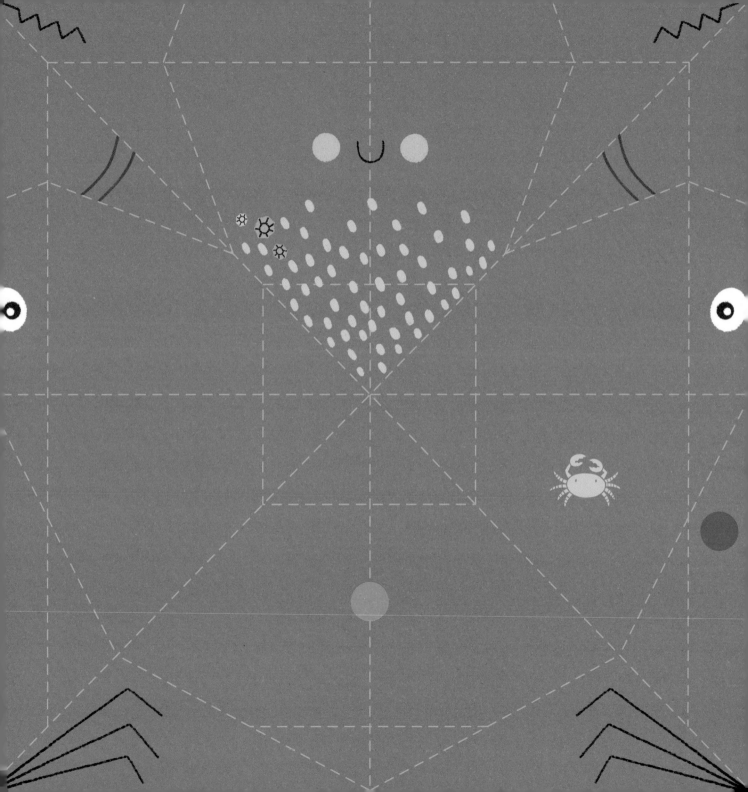

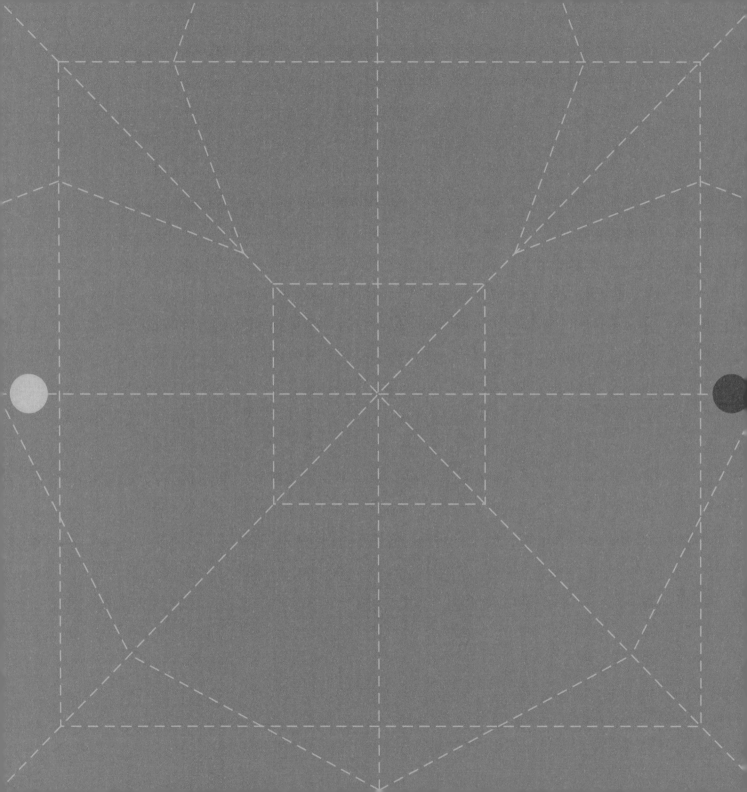

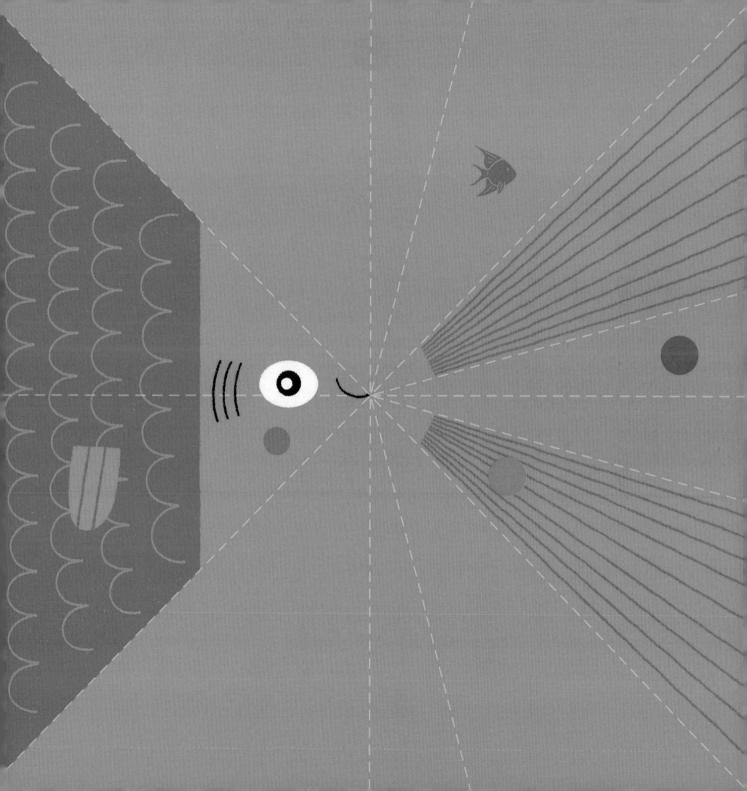

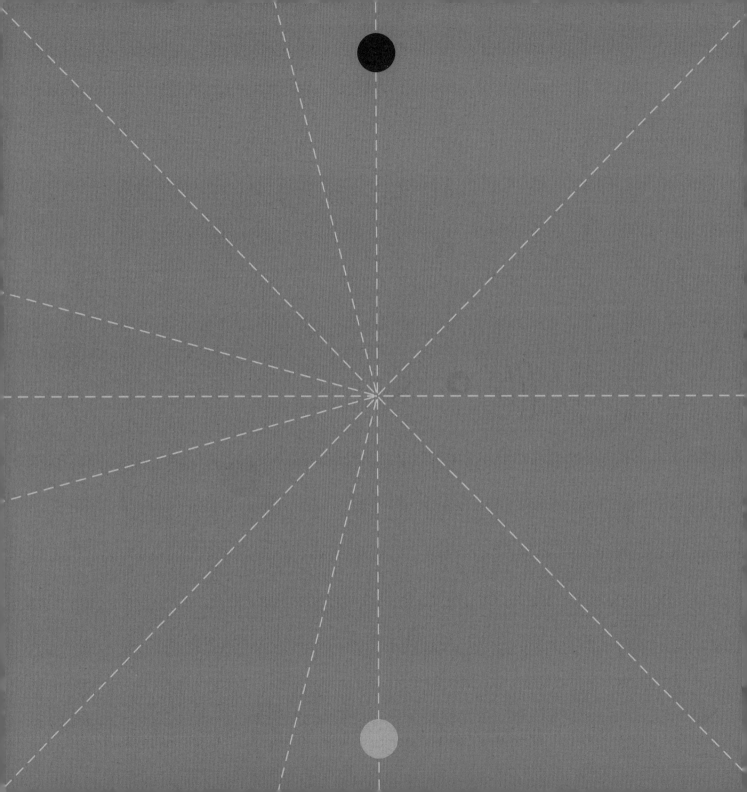

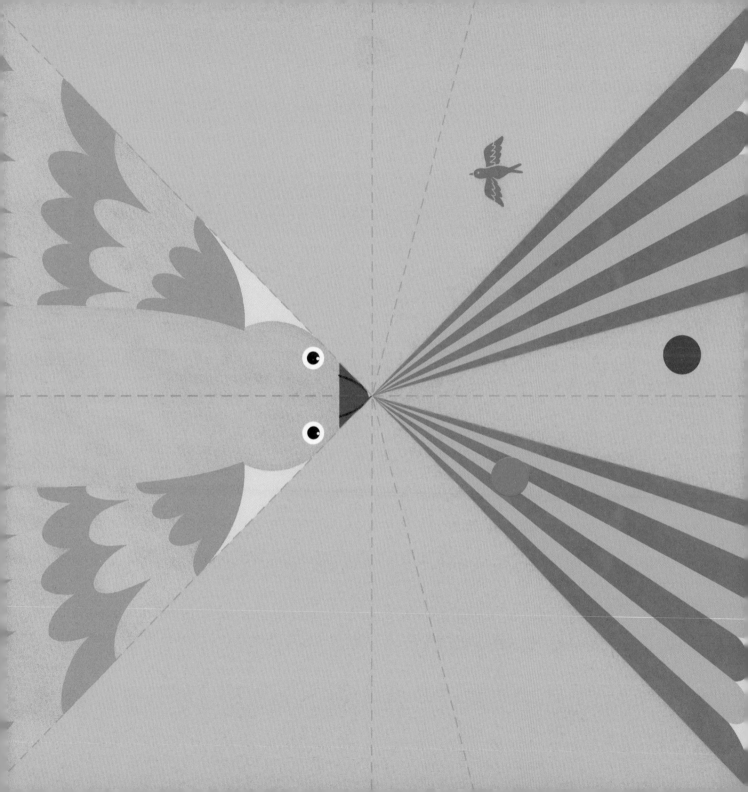

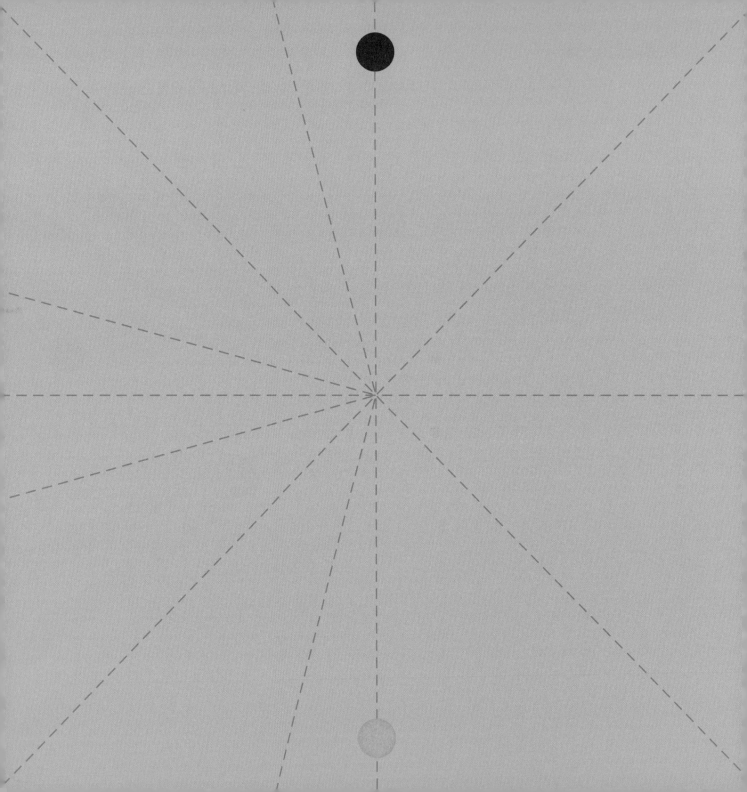

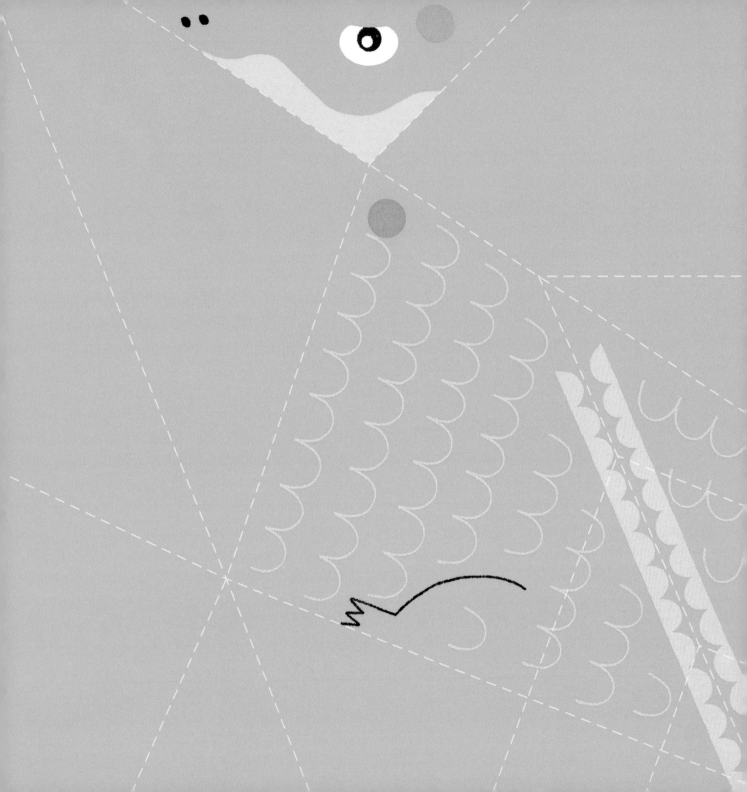

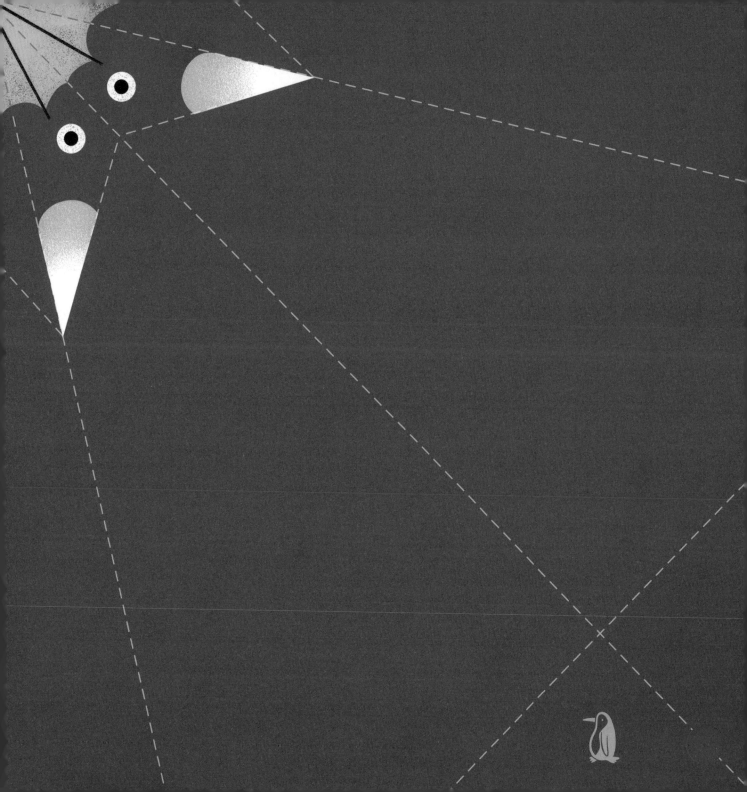

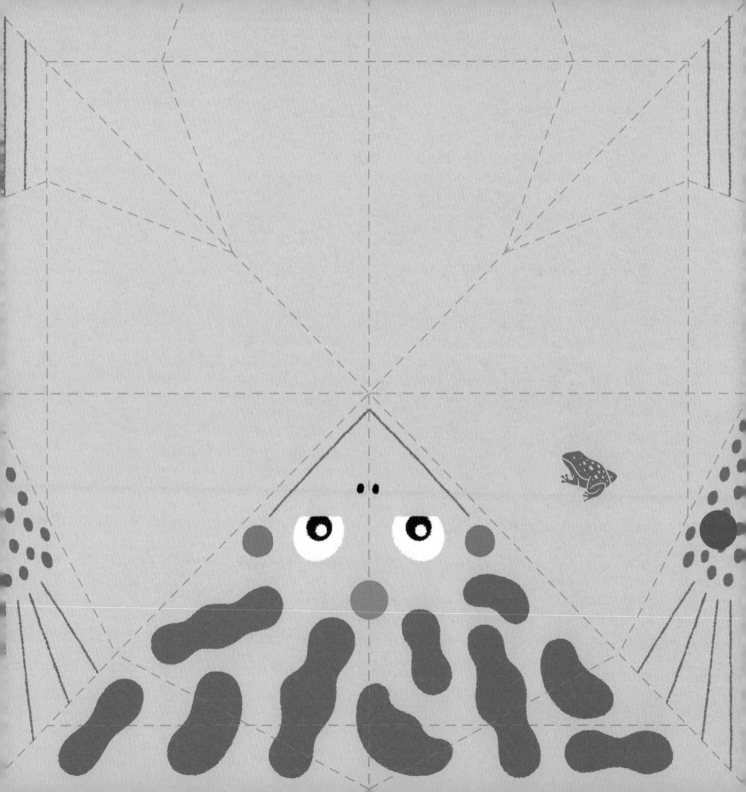

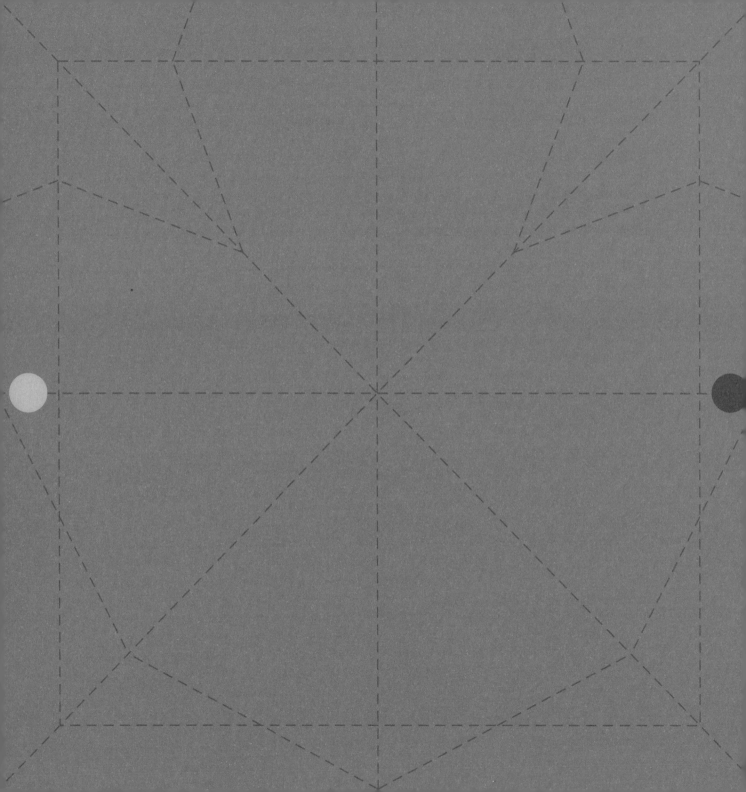

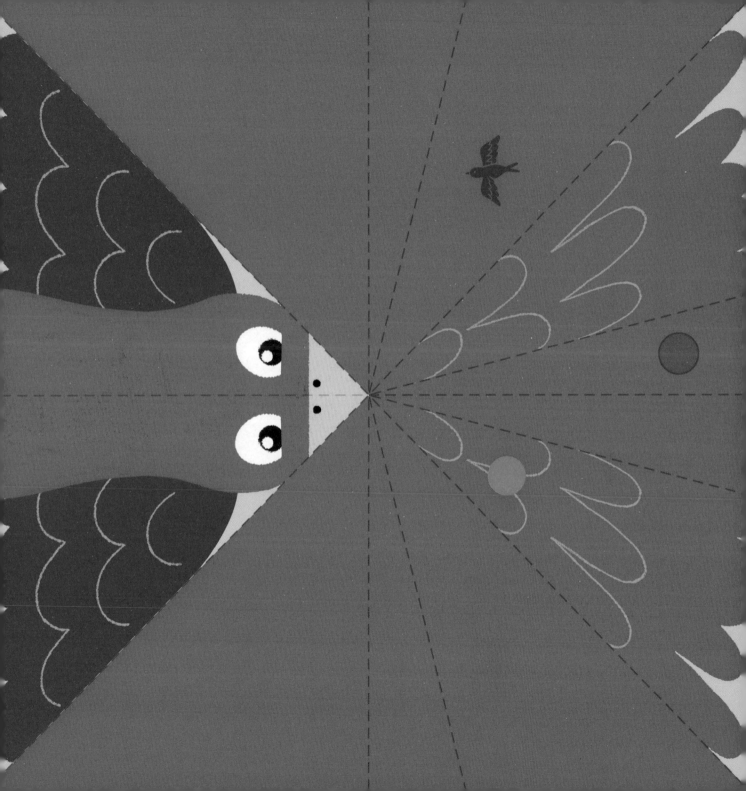

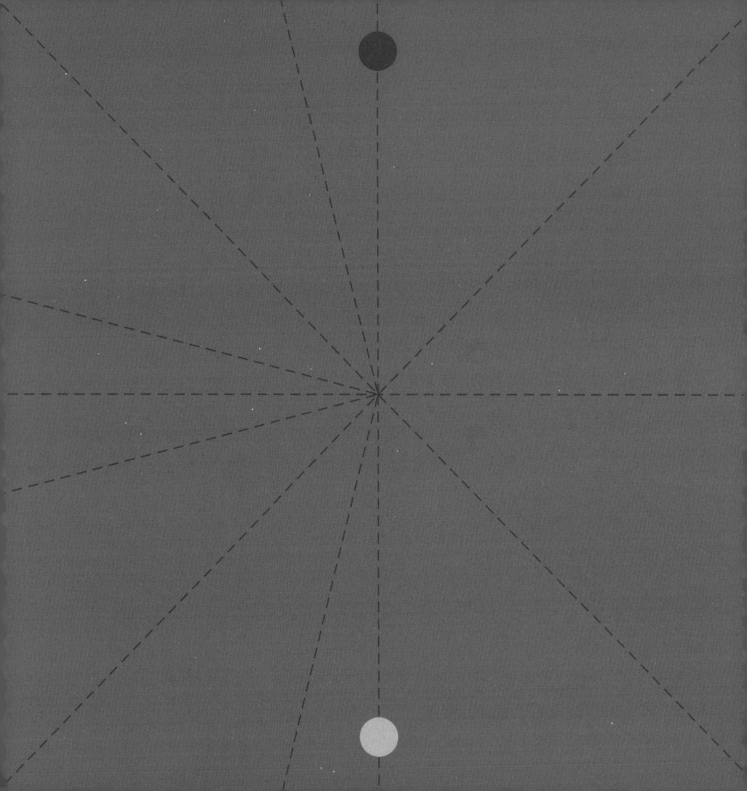

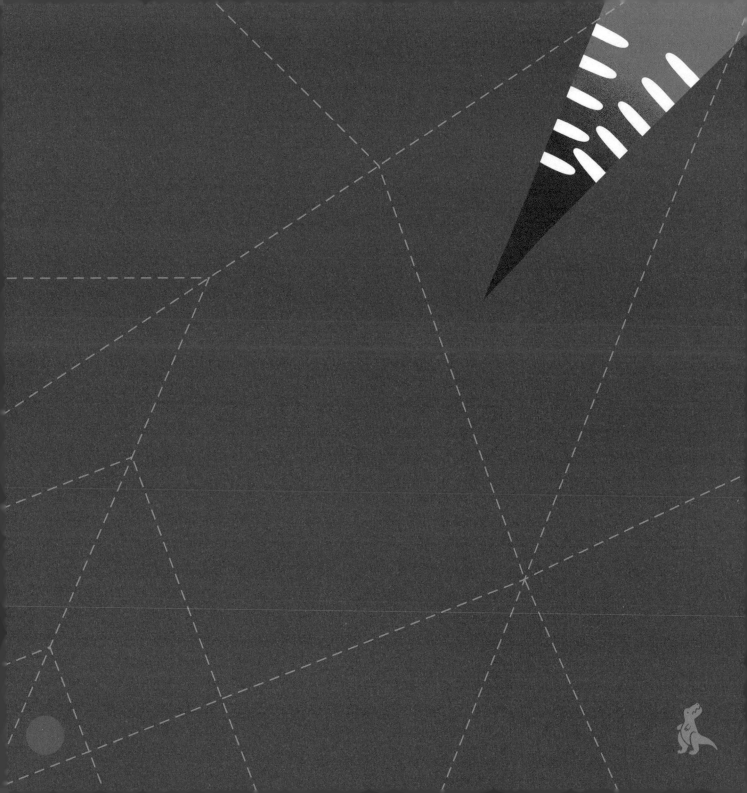

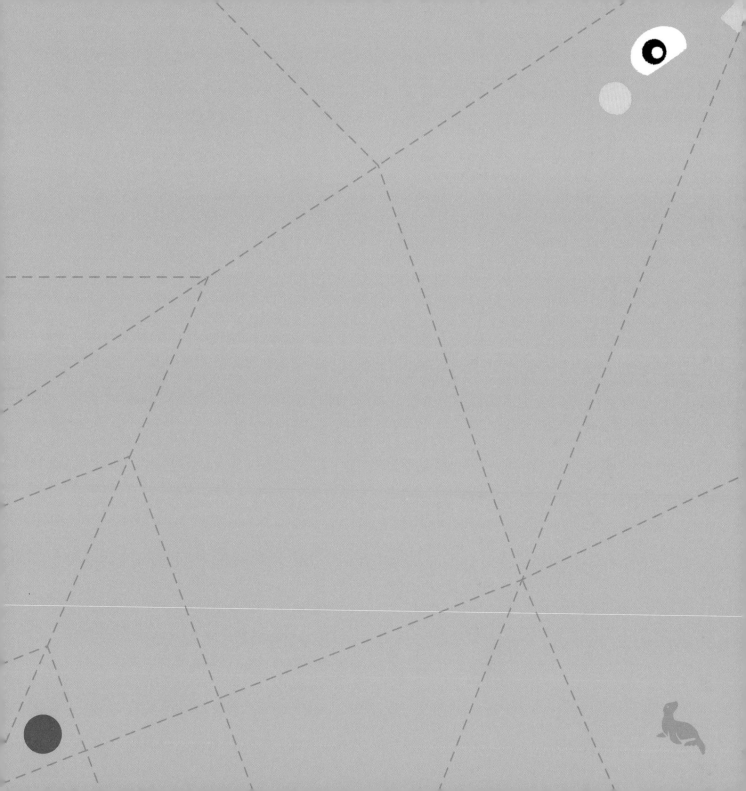

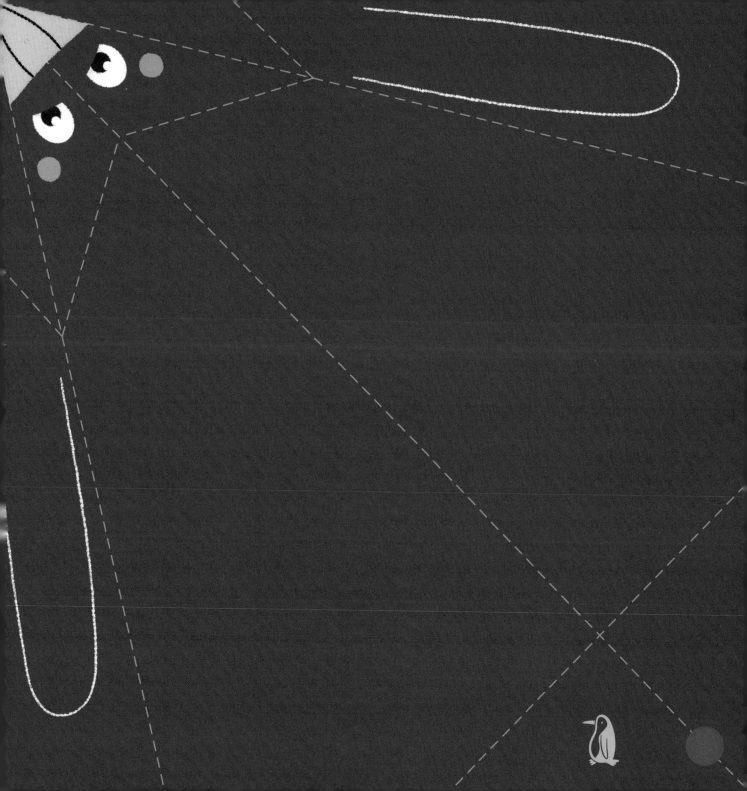

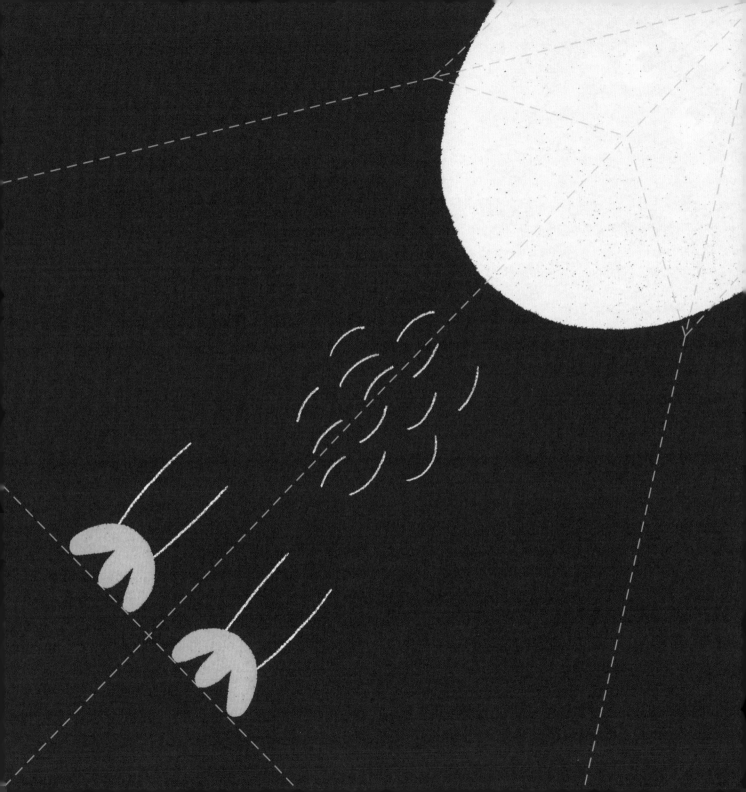

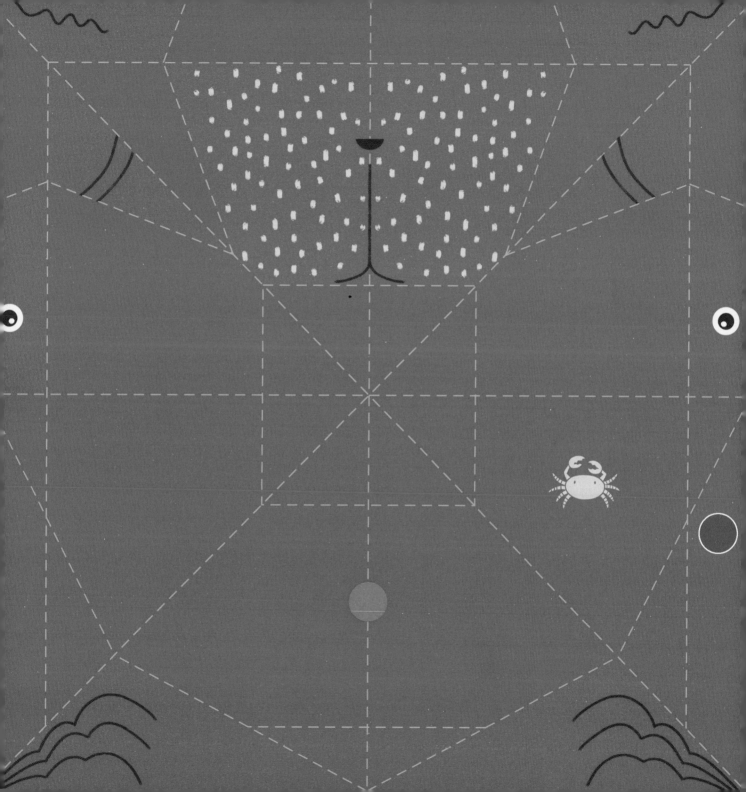

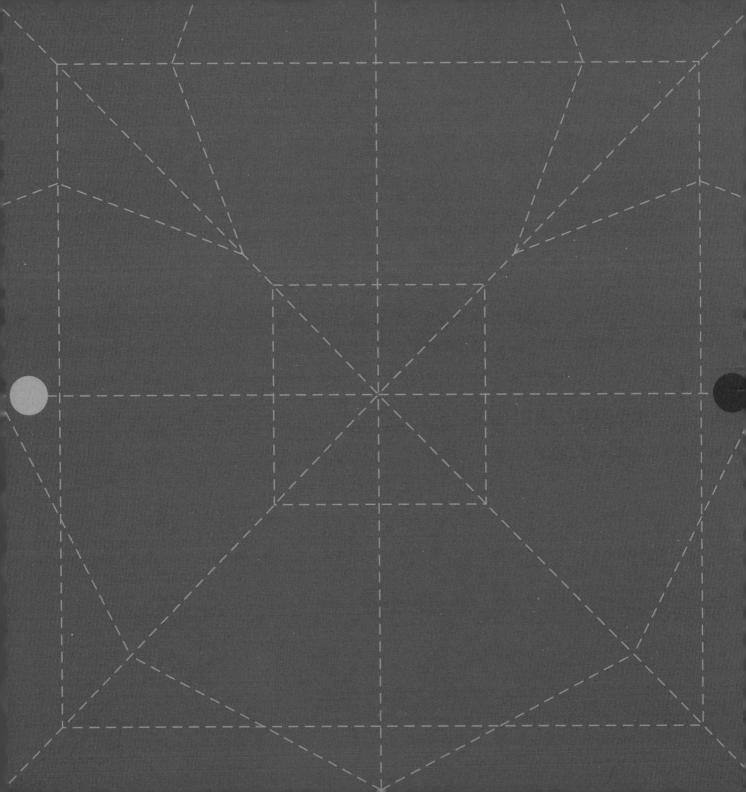

   # To fold the Seal, Crocodile or Dinosaur...

...choose a pull-out page with any of these animal pictures on it, then follow the instructions below.

1

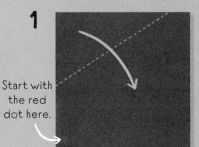

Start with the red dot here.

Fold down this corner of the paper along the dotted line.

2

Then, fold in this corner along the dotted line.

3

Next, fold up this corner along the dotted line.

4

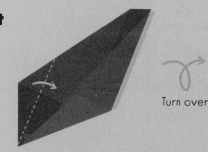

Turn over

Fold in this corner along the dotted line, to make a point.

5

The yellow dot should be here.

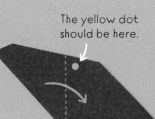

Fold the top point along the dotted line, like this.

6

Your animal's face will show here.

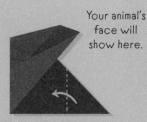

Then, fold in this point along the dotted line, to make a tail.

7

Fold back the tip of the tail, like this.

Your finished model will look like this.

Seal, Dinosaur or Crocodile

Scan this QR code to access videos showing you how to fold the Seal, Crocodile or Dinosaur.

To fold the Penguin or Whale...

...choose a pull-out page with any of these animal pictures on it, then follow the instructions below.

1

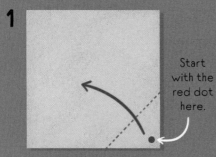

Start with the red dot here.

Fold up this bottom corner along the dotted line.

2

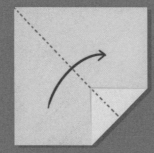

Fold along this dotted line, to fold the paper in half.

3

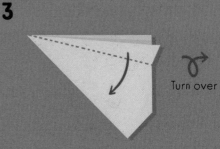

Turn over

Fold down just the top layer of paper, along this dotted line.

4

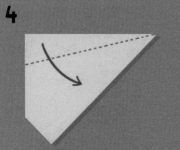

Fold down the top corner along this dotted line.

5

Fold all the layers together.

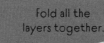
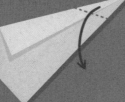

Fold down the top point along this dotted line, then unfold it again.

6

Flap down the entire front half, to open out the model.

7 Grasp the point with finger and thumb.

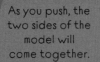

As you push, the two sides of the model will come together.

Hold the model up off the table. Push the top point down.

8

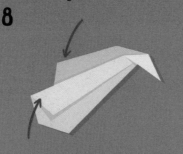

Push these corners together to flatten the model. Flatten all the folds again with your thumbnail.

Your finished model will look like this.

Penguin   Whale

Scan this QR code to access videos showing you how to fold the Penguin or Whale.

To fold the Fish, Bird or Butterfly...

...choose a pull-out page with any of these animal pictures on it, then follow the instructions below.

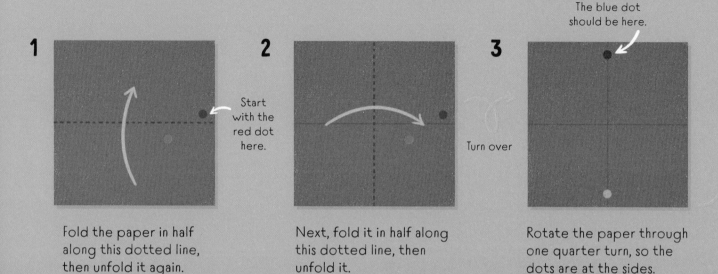

1

Fold the paper in half along this dotted line, then unfold it again.

Start with the red dot here.

2

Next, fold it in half along this dotted line, then unfold it.

Turn over

3

The blue dot should be here.

Rotate the paper through one quarter turn, so the dots are at the sides.

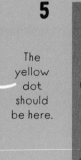

4

Fold it from corner to corner like this, then unfold it again.

The yellow dot should be here.

5

Next, fold it from corner to corner like this, then unfold it.

6

As you push, the model will flatten.

You will now have a shape like this. Push in here, so the blue and yellow dots meet.

7 Rotate the top of the model away from you.

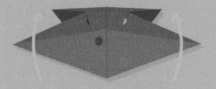

Next, flatten into a triangle, so the red and green dots are on top.

8

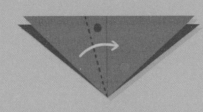

Take hold of the side with the red dot. Fold just the top layer along the dotted line.

9

Take hold of the side with the green dot. Fold the top layer over, along the dotted line.

For Fish or Bird, turn over

Fish or Bird

Butterfly

Your finished model will look like this.

Scan this QR code to access videos showing you how to fold the Fish, Bird or Butterfly.

To fold the Crab, Bug or Frog...

...choose a pull-out page with any of these animal pictures on it, then follow the instructions below.

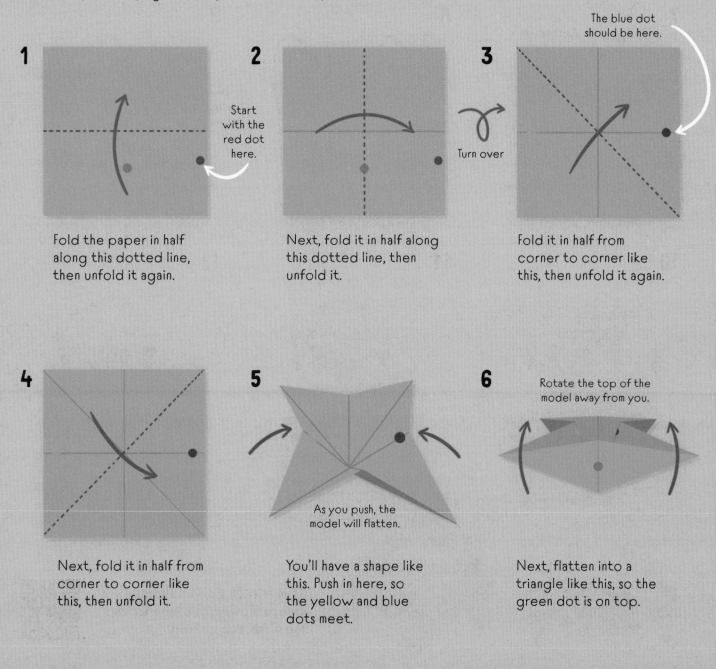

1

Fold the paper in half along this dotted line, then unfold it again.

Start with the red dot here.

2

Next, fold it in half along this dotted line, then unfold it.

Turn over

3

The blue dot should be here.

Fold it in half from corner to corner like this, then unfold it again.

4

Next, fold it in half from corner to corner like this, then unfold it.

5

As you push, the model will flatten.

You'll have a shape like this. Push in here, so the yellow and blue dots meet.

6

Rotate the top of the model away from you.

Next, flatten into a triangle like this, so the green dot is on top.

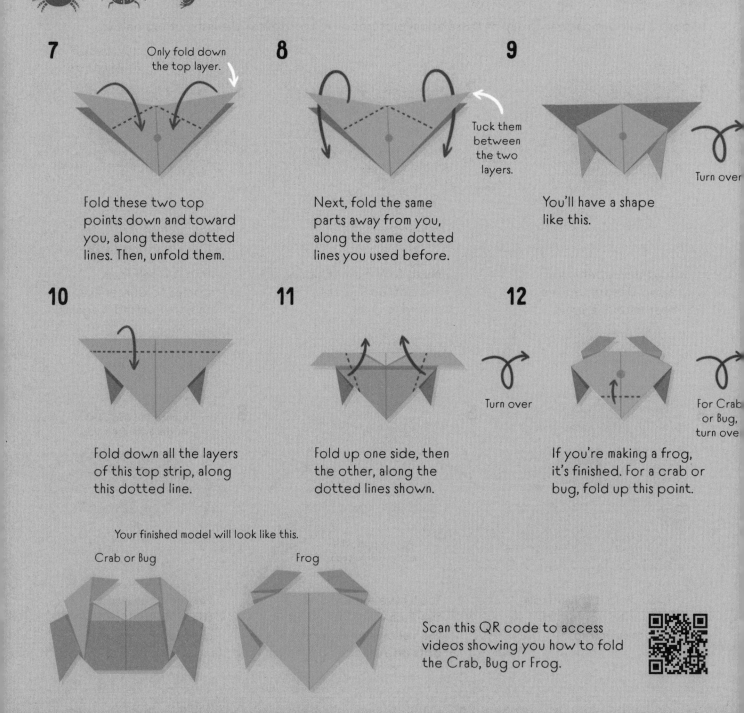

7

Only fold down the top layer.

Fold these two top points down and toward you, along these dotted lines. Then, unfold them.

8

Tuck them between the two layers.

Next, fold the same parts away from you, along the same dotted lines you used before.

9

Turn over

You'll have a shape like this.

10

Fold down all the layers of this top strip, along this dotted line.

11

Turn over

Fold up one side, then the other, along the dotted lines shown.

12

For Crab or Bug, turn ove

If you're making a frog, it's finished. For a crab or bug, fold up this point.

Your finished model will look like this.

Crab or Bug

Frog

Scan this QR code to access videos showing you how to fold the Crab, Bug or Frog.